Rehabilitation of the Physically Handicapped Adolescent

Hilda K. Waldhorn

ATION
F THE
APPED
SCENT

This book is directed to all nonmedical personnel who counsel the physically handicapped adolescent and guide him toward his psychological and physical rehabilitation: counselors, social workers, psychologists, teachers, parents. The author offers information on epilepsy, hemophilia, sickle cell anemia, diabetes, allergies, and brain injury— all within the framework of the rehabilitative process.

Describing some of the new and exciting techniques that have been developed by the medical, psychiatric and teaching professions, this book fills an important gap in the national effort to help handicapped adolescents realize their abilities, and achieve their full potential. The ideas and suggestions presented are the results of the author's clinical experience, observation and careful evaluation in the course of her work. They offer reassurance and practical guidance to all those who work with these youngsters.

The John Day Company
New York

Rehabilitation of the Physically Handicapped Adolescent

HILDA K. WALDHORN

JOHN DAY BOOKS IN

SPECIAL EDUCATION

The John Day Company

NEW YORK | AN **Intext** PUBLISHER

Library of Congress Cataloging in Publication Data

Waldhorn, Hilda K
  Rehabilitation of the physically handicapped adolescent.

  Bibliography:
    1. Physically handicapped—Rehabilitation. I. Title. [DNLM:
  1. Counseling—In adolescence. 2. Handicapped. 3. Rehabilitation—In
  adolescence.
  HD7255 W163r 1973 (P)]
  HV3011.W27   362.4   72-2420
  ISBN: 0-381-98193-2

The John Day Company, 257 Park Avenue South, New York, N.Y. 10010

Published on the same day in Canada by Longman Canada Limited.

Printed in the United States of America

TO

ALL HANDICAPPED

ADOLESCENTS

HILDA K. WALDHORN was until recently Coordinator of the High School Homebound Program of the Federation of the Handicapped, New York City, a prevocational evaluation program for students on home instruction. She has also worked as psychological and vocational counselor at Polytechnic Institute of Brooklyn, New York.

Contents

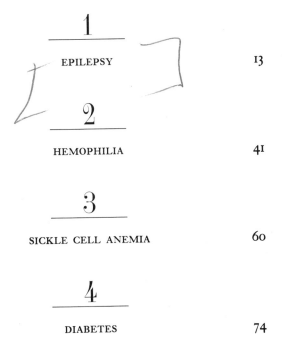

Foreword

Disability strikes tens of thousands of young people each year. In the past, such young people encountered innumerable problems in developing careers, obtaining a suitable education, establishing families, and becoming part of their communities. Today, these difficulties are less formidable than they once were, due largely to the work of organizations such as Federation of the Handicapped and gifted workers such as Hilda Waldhorn.

New techniques have been developed by educators and behavioral scientists that help disabled young people to make the most of their abilities. Simultaneously, social action on behalf of the handicapped is promoting improved attitudes toward, and opportunities for, the handicapped. The net effect of this two-pronged attack on the problem is producing gratifying results. More than ever, disabled young people are acquiring the skills needed to function in our society, and more than ever our society is encouraging them to use these skills without restriction. It is reassuring to those of us who serve the disabled to note that not only are they gaining access to jobs in the community, but, in many cases, they are achieving positions of leadership and distinction.

This book fills an important gap in the national effort to help handicapped young people to realize their potential. It is a well-organized effort by Mrs. Waldhorn to synthesize her extensive knowledge and experience into a meaningful presentation that can help handicapped students, their parents, their teachers and counselors, and their neighbors to understand the problem more fully and to take constructive steps to deal with it. In the past, some of this information was available—but not in the convenient and readable form that characterizes this book.

It is a source of great pleasure to me that many of the ideas presented were generated and tested at Federation of the Handicapped. Thus, it may be assumed that they have a practicality born of clinical observation and careful evaluation. Obviously, no two handicapped young people are the same. However, there are similarities that suggest that the principles set forth by the author have great applicability. Through accepting these principles and applying them on an individual basis, workers for the handicapped will inevitably improve their performance. If this occurs, this book will be respected not only for its scholarly excellence but for its practical guidance to youth workers as well.

Milton Cohen, *Executive Director*
Federation of the Handicapped

Introduction

My intended audience is composed of all nonmedical personnel who counsel the physically handicapped adolescent and guide him toward rehabilitation. My hope is that the information presented here will help rehabilitation counselors, social workers, psychologists, and teachers to answer the urgent queries the handicapped adolescent puts about his disability and about how he can learn best to live with it. And because the handicapped adolescent and his parents must understand both the dimensions of the handicap and the importance of cooperation in the struggle against that handicap, I hope that they too will find useful information and usable insights.

The handicaps discussed in this book—epilepsy, hemophilia, sickle cell anemia, diabetes mellitus, allergy, bronchial asthma, and brain injury—were selected because little or nothing about them is available in the literature of rehabilitation of handicapped adolescents. Almost all information about hemophilia, epilepsy, and sickle cell anemia, for example, is confined to professional medical journals and texts. Only recently has epilepsy been included as a chapter in a text designed for special education courses. And although brain injury has been written about extensively, the writings have often been prohibitively specialized. My aim has been to make accessible to all who are intimately concerned with the rehabilitation of those afflicted with these disabilities both the basic medical knowledge (along with some indication of the latest scientific advances, many of them dramatic and historic) and the most acceptable rehabilitative procedures.

Toward this end I have structured each chapter to include *medical data:* definition of the disease, its symptoms, etiology, care, and prognosis; and *rehabilitation patterns:* case histories that stress (without violating confidentiality) the psychological problems frequently coincident with the medical. A companion volume, *Rehabilitation of the Psychologically Handicapped Adolescent*, is being planned along similar lines.

I owe thanks to many who have helped me. I have drawn freely from the excellent, comprehensive materials published by the various foundations dedicated to the handicaps described here. Kay Hamalian and Dr. Bernard Stillerman contributed pertinent materials. Terry Morrison, Beth Hart, Sylvia Rothenberg, Valerie Auerbach, and Stephen Waldhorn commented perceptively and encouraged me. I wish to thank Dr. Louis Aledorf for his helpful reading of the chapter on hemophilia. Rhea Tabakin's assistance with the footnotes was indispensable. Finally, special thanks to my husband, Arthur, who listened, read, and counseled.

Hilda K. Waldhorn
New York

1

Epilepsy

The history of the definition and treatment of epilepsy from ancient times until the 1930's is a record of man's most perverse superstitions and near diabolical distortions. For some ancients, epilepsy was a sacred disease that the gods visited upon chosen mortals. Hercules was such an epileptic, as was King Saul. For many others, epilepsy was a visitation by demons, who might be released through a hole drilled in the skull. Only Hippocrates in the fourth century B.C. stood boldly aloof from such nonsense, arguing that epilepsy was an organic, not a divine affliction. But the demonologists and the witch-mongers triumphed until the nineteenth century. Even so, scientific knowledge lagged—and when the doctors remain ignorant, the layman clings to old wives' tales.

Thus Fëdor Dostoevski, an epileptic, believed in folk remedies recommended by his family. His doctors were no more scientific than his family in their treatment. One recommended bloodletting, another marriage, and a third, astrologically oriented, warned of asphyxiation during the period of the new moon. Their understanding of the causes of his illness veered as far from the mark. One physician linked Dostoevski's epilepsy to the trauma of his witnessing his father's murder; another thought his seizures to be the result of brutal treatment while he was in prison. Had Dostoevski traveled through Europe or America as late as 1910, he might have heard from other doctors such reasons as overwork, criminal impulses, or debauchery, that he had worms in his intestines, or a defect in his endocrine glands. Although Dostoevski humorously referred to his seizures as "kondrashkas with a little breeze,"[1] he was also vulnerable to the false beliefs of his time and suffered agonies fearing that he was insane, that his memory was failing, or that his mind was deteriorating.

The truth about epilepsy could not be told before it was known, or before public sentiment was ready to discard ancient taboos and false beliefs. Medical texts, encyclopedias, and psychiatric reports as late as the 1930's classified epilepsy as an inherited, incurable, hopeless disease of unknown cause—an illness from which society must be protected. Since then, however, science has solved the mysteries and calmed the spirits of the unholy past. Entries in reference books began to become more cautious. Instead of repeating false myths, they referred to a vague, chronic nervous ailment of unknown causes, treated with bromides and barbiturates.

Two major scientific discoveries in the 1930's dramatically and abruptly contradicted more than 2,000 years of unfounded myth. In 1935 the most refined technique of diagnosis to date became available. A machine known as the EEG (electroencephalograph) recorded the electrical currents that are constantly being generated in tiny amounts in the brains of all individuals and delineated distinct patterns of electrical tracings from grand mal and petit mal seizures—the two most common forms of epilepsy (*A Patient's Guide* n.d.). This major breakthrough was followed almost immediately in 1937 by the discovery of the drug Dilantin,[2] which by itself or together with phenobarbital effectively controls seizures. Now, there is nothing devilish or malevolent about excessive electrical discharge in an injured portion of the brain. Confronted with medical facts and truths in place of medieval fantasy, doctors, educators, epileptics, their families, and all members of society had suddenly to discount and unlearn all the old prejudicial dogma. But prejudice dies hard, and an urgent need remains today to speak these truths loud and spread them fast so that they may more quickly narrow the gap between knowledge and practice.

Total clarity of understanding about epilepsy is still not ours, but the most recent medical texts have made considerable progress toward illuminating all aspects of epilepsy. Despite the variety of descriptions of epilepsy as a "condition," a "symptom," a "disease," a "seizure," or not an illness at all, but an "accusation," we know definitely now that epilepsy is an organic disorder of the brain and has to do with injured brain cells. It is an irritative reaction that occurs in the form of an attack when the orderly electrical activity of the brain cells is disrupted, and electrical energy is discharged too fast. Attacks may take as many different forms as there are brain cells, depending upon the location of the malfunctioning cells and the extent of the injury. (Barrows and Goldensohn n.d.).

Having fixed the locus of epilepsy in the brain, we should hasten to add that although epilepsy is a brain disorder, it is *not* a "mental illness." Patients will not know whether they are physically or mentally ill unless it is clearly explained to them that epilepsy is a physical disorder involving sick nerve cells. Only when it becomes common public knowledge that epilepsy is a medical problem concerning malfunctioning brain cells will we become immune to the old misleading notions. Furthermore, having accepted the fact that epilepsy is a disorder of cells in the brain, it becomes easier to understand the underlying physical basis for so many different kinds of seizures that patients experience. Because there are billions of cells in the brain, seizures vary in form depending upon the specific functions of the particular irritated cells. It is little wonder that attempts to classify or categorize types of attacks have led to needless confusion.

Nevertheless, the three most common types of epilepsy—petit mal, psychomotor and grand mal—have yielded to a more orderly description.[3]

Twenty to 30 percent of all epileptics report experience with petit mal, the "little sickness."[4] Momentary blankness and pauses in the activity—the symptoms of

petit mal—frequently pass unnoticed or, in some instances, are attributed to daydreams, inattention, or
behavior problems. Another 10 percent of all epileptics
experience psychomotor epilepsy, which is sometimes
accompanied by unusual or peculiar behavior. The patient is, for example, unaware of what he is doing for a
few minutes. Both types, however, regardless of severity
and frequency, require thorough physical and neurological examination in order to obtain the best possible program of treatment and to prevent their developing into
grand mal. Between 65 and 70 percent of all epileptic
cases are grand mal—the "big sickness," in which the
person usually loses consciousness, falls, and has convulsions. To the worried bystander, a grand mal seizure
appears violent and painful—but it soon runs its course
and comes to a quiet end.[5] The patient may immediately
resume activities, or he may wish first to rest.

There is general agreement in the medical profession
about the two main diagnostic categories based on suspected cause: in *symptomatic epilepsy*, the cause is known;
in *idiopathic epilepsy*, the cause cannot be determined by
present diagnostic methods. Since the causes of epilepsy
vary as widely as the manifestation of symptoms, epilepsy is particularly difficult to define and understand as
a single disease. Seizures are symptomatic in many illnesses and are due to many different causes. For the most
part, however, seizures are a result of physiological disturbances or physical injuries—head or birth injury, infection of the central nervous system, insufficient oxygen passed to the brain, brain tumor, virus infections, or
other body chemistry problems.[6]

It is generally accepted that an hereditary tendency or

predisposition toward attacks does exist—but opinions differ about whether or not epilepsy itself is inherited (Sands and Seaver 1966: 6). Instead of the 1 in 200 chances that normal parents will have an epileptic child, the epileptic person with a normal mate has 1 chance out of 40 of having an epileptic child. However, the possibility of inheriting epilepsy is rarely a significant deterrent to marriage or having children.

Some disagreement also exists concerning the relationship of epilepsy to emotional problems but it has not been demonstrated that there is any direct cause and effect pattern between epilepsy and psychological disturbances. Nor has a clearly identifiable "epileptic personality" been delineated (Goldensohn and Barrows n.d.: 20). Psychological or emotional problems of adjustment are more likely to arise because the epileptic person has been alienated and wrongly judged "insane" or "retarded." True, some seizures may be brought on by frustration, emotionally charged situations, boredom, and inactivity. But we must remember that it is the injured cells that cause the seizures under these circumstances, not the circumstances themselves or the victim's psychological makeup.

Although epilepsy is the most discriminated against, it is the least disabling of all handicaps. The epileptic person is not so permanently handicapped as one who suffers from cerebral palsy, orthopedic disability, chronic illness, or retardation. There is nothing static about epilepsy; in fact, it is a highly changeable condition. Although it afflicts children, it sometimes disappears with maturity. It varies in form and intensity with each person and at different times. With medical management, vocational training, and special placement, the epileptic is no longer disabled. It has been amply demonstrated that the vast majority can learn, can be trained, and can hold jobs as efficiently as their seizure-free peers.[7] The life expectancy of the epileptic is good and his hereditary factor is slight. In fact, most persons with epilepsy are much like everyone else. They can develop and learn as well as their peers within the limits of their individual capacities. Their intellectual potential ranges as broadly as that of normal children. Some are above average, some average, some below average, and, as in any group, a few fall far below average and cannot be educated. Emotional disturbance can be located in the epileptic precisely as in the physically normal. Modern medicine and improved diagnostic techniques developed during the past thirty years have made it possible for 50 percent of those with grand mal—the most severe form—to be completely seizure-free and still another 30 percent to be adequately controlled so that they may live normal, productive lives; 80 percent of all forms of epilepsy can be effectively treated with medication. Fewer than 20 percent of those with very severe convulsions are unemployable, and many of those may work in a sheltered environment.

Why, then, do only 20 percent of the two million epileptic children in our country seek or get help? (*Epilepsy* 1967: 3). Largely because they have surrendered to the greatest single enemy confronting the epileptic—social prejudice. We must help them combat and conquer that foe. And we must begin by saying No to the fallacy of past myths and refusing even to whisper damaging untruths. It is not the devil but an imbalance in electrochemical reactions in the brain that causes sudden loss of consciousness, brief or prolonged. The protests of specialists in rehabilitation and epileptics themselves must also be heard. Epileptics must claim their right to live decent lives. They must register with the far too few epileptic clinics in our country (about eighty) for one of more than a dozen medicines that can decrease the frequency and severity of attacks. They must give the lie to the false and cruel innuendoes of "feeblemindedness" and "craziness" by perfecting their skills while fostering good mental health. And they must demonstrate again and again that they can be rehabilitated and gainfully employed. Finally, all of us must erase the insult to the epileptic made humiliatingly explicit in outmoded laws that exist in thirteen states—laws that restrict epileptics in marriage, childbearing, immigration, and the right to drive a car. Some states even require sterilization.[8]

The tragedy of the unredeemed lives of epileptic youngsters is documented in case studies. Far too often epileptics are crushed after years of rejection by harassed and befuddled parents, by frightened teachers and prejudiced neighbors—all ignorant of the facts about and treatment of epilepsy. Together, they have thwarted a human being from his right to live by failing to guide him even to the first door—medical aid—opening to the world of self-fulfillment.

Mary Ann

Mary Ann was such a person—a pretty but pathetically confused and helpless girl of seventeen whose seizures before and, unhappily, after two years of rehabilitative efforts remained undiagnosed and untreated. When Mary Ann first entered an evaluative program, she was confused about her "spells." She could not answer questions about medication. "For what?" she asked. She did not know when her attacks had first started, how often they occurred, or even what happened during a seizure. She was even surprised that she should be asked about such things. She was also bewildered about how she should behave. Obviously, Mary Ann did not have the slightest idea that she suffered from epileptic seizures, what they were, or what might be done to help her—and, understandably, she had developed psychologically unhealthy symptoms and patterns of coping. Not clear about what was expected of her, she honestly tried on many occasions to please but succeeded only in stirring mischief.

She disappeared from the rehabilitative vocational evaluation program for weeks on end, phoning her counselor with unbelievably complicated excuses: "Like, I can't come in today because I have nothing to wear and my mother won't buy me anything . . . she buys my sisters and brothers everything but when I have a spell and fall and tear my skirt, she won't get me another one . . . or if I get holes in my shoes because I walk so much because I can't sleep she won't get me a new pair or give me the money to take my clothes out of the cleaners." Incidentally, she arrived an hour later that day toting a bag of old clothes and worn shoes "just to prove to you that I'm not lying." On another occasion, after weeks of not attending, Mary Ann phoned to report: "I have a doctor's appointment tomorrow, but I am not calling to have you remind me to keep it, because I can't go anyway but I can't tell you why because it's personal."

All that was consistent about Mary Ann's behavior was her expectation of punishment. Whether she did right or wrong, whether the response to her behavior was approving or not, Mary Ann always apologized—for not coming on time, for coming on time, for causing so much trouble, for having seizures, for wanting a job, for getting it, for doing well on the job, for borrowing money, for paying it back. Quite simply, Mary Ann was apologizing for being alive. After all, she may have reasoned, her brother had obligingly died six months earlier of *his* spells.[9]

On and off for two years, Mary Ann mourned her brother and apologized, broke appointments that had been set up for her at the hospital clinic and promises to keep her vocational and therapy schedules. After several attempts to involve her parents, it became clear that they too had "given up" along with Mary Ann.

Those who fail to seek and obtain medical care remain vulnerable at best, and, at worst, helpless in the grip of their seizures—lost and confused. Lacking guidelines to follow, they grow miserable, frightened, and angry. Many withdraw into fantasy, hallucinations, and delusions of grandeur in order to avoid the full impact of total rejection as unwanted children. However, such extreme instances are becoming the exception. A happier turn of events is more likely as doctors, parents, teachers, and counselors acquire fuller understanding about epilepsy and can offer assistance more readily at the first sign of trouble.

John

John suffered petit mal seizures (cause unknown) but was helped to obtain medical advice and treatment. At seventeen, John's barely discernible moments of "blankness and staring" distressed and perplexed him. He had become secretive and defensive lest others discover his "queerness." Intent upon concealing or minimizing his condition, he was uncooperative with doctors and denied any fears, but stubbornly refused to travel by himself. Though his work was erratic—he skipped whole lines while reading, became disorganized when filing, and often pretended he had accurately completed the task—he blamed others for his inadequate performance.

His parents always treated John as if something disastrous were about to happen should he go to school alone or travel with friends on the "dangerous" subways. Nor did they allow him to stay at home alone. Horrified at the word "epilepsy," they never directly explained to John what was wrong but consulted with others behind his back. John grew frightened by all of this mysterious behavior and increasingly depended upon his parents. Fortunately, he did not unreservedly accept the submissive role imposed upon him. He very much wanted more independence to travel, greater freedom to make friends, and an opportunity to prepare for a job. Although John had often listened to other students discuss their particular handicaps, he had never volunteered information about himself, insisting only, "I have no problems." As job possibilities became real for him, he mustered the courage to estimate how his "spells" might affect his chances for employment. As he was encouraged to hope and plan, he became less fearful of both his individual therapist's explorations and of group therapy. The day came when he told the group, "You know, I have seizures too, Mary Ann, and I've been ashamed to speak about them before or to admit it because I was afraid people wouldn't understand or like me anymore. I think I was afraid to admit it because my mother always tells me not to tell anyone about my spells—I guess she's been afraid of them too."

From that point, it was only a short step to put John in touch with a nearby teen-age clinic and to talk to him about some of the tests and medicines the clinic might use for diagnosis and treatment. When he learned that effective medical treatment was available, he insisted upon receiving it, despite the apprehension of his parents. John benefited considerably from the comprehensive medical and neurological examination and treatment plan. A month or two later he delightedly told the group that he was having fewer spells. He began to accept the challenge of traveling and, soon after, began to earn money on a part-time job doing filing and interoffice messenger work. Thereafter, he insisted upon paying for his own expenses and clothes. Freed of past restrictions and oppressive uncertainties, he laughed at his old fears and settled down to the serious task of an honest assessment of his skills for future training possibilities. John's wholesome decision to live a richer life, together with the combined efforts of a rehabilitative and medical team, brought him the assurance of medical stability for his seizures.

Countless youngsters with epilepsy have struggled to adjust to self, family, and society. Let's consider the heroic efforts of some of these young people, for it is recognition of their accomplishments that will destroy the false stigma attached to epilepsy.

Helen

Helen didn't look much like a trailblazer when she was interviewed at the outset of her year's attendance in a rehabilitation program. But her story demonstrates the dogged perseverance and steadfastness essential for any handicapped person determined to live a healthier and happier existence. Initially she was a frail, plain-looking girl of eighteen who spoke hesitantly and only occasionally ventured a weak half-smile. She looked unhappy and withdrawn, though she denied having any problems. Diagnosed as suffering grand mal seizures resulting from a birth trauma, Helen admitted only, "I have blackouts . . . that's all." Yet she had spent most of her days alone on home instruction[10] with no opportunity for making friends. Her regular trips to the doctor and constant reminders to take her medicine had convinced her that she was "different." She was socially gauche, shy, and immature in her relationships with boys and girls her own age. Shortly after she began attending the program, she seemed to realize how much she had missed and how lonely she had been. As if to make up for lost time, she childishly and impulsively threw herself upon the other boys and girls, trying to possess them as her special friends. She called all the boys her "boy friend" and overwhelmed the girls with endless flattery.

Helen's parents were basically warm, decent people

much interested in helping her, and they rightly encouraged her to be as physically active as possible. However, they were as unrealistic as she about vocational goals and her very real limitations. Unaware of the problems she would most certainly have to face on any job, they smiled approvingly when Helen spoke of wanting to become a nurse. At the same time, they discouraged her from riding alone on buses or subways and endearingly referred to her as being "retarded."

Tests showed that despite considerable brain damage, Helen had average ability on some tasks. The epileptic, one must remember, is not retarded. When intelligence testing of the epileptic produces lower scores, a variety of reasons must be examined: organic damage is a possibility, of course, but so too are the effects of certain medications, gaps in education, absence of those daily living experiences that foster social intelligence, and even a lack of experience in taking tests. Helen did very poorly on a variety of tasks designed to assess vocational skills, thereby eliminating a wide range of possibilities in vocational training. However, she was extraordinarily competent at simple, repetitive, assembly-type work. Initially, Helen could not understand instructions and worked very slowly. However, she carefully and patiently completed her work and she always was polite and cooperative in her relationships with the work supervisors.

In individual and group therapy, Helen gradually learned to relate more appropriately to the other boys and girls. She tempered her advances and soon realized that others were as eager for reasonable companionship as she. Before long, they wished to visit one another's homes or to plan shopping trips. Helen had her own money, for her work had improved and qualified her for workshop wages.[11] When she brought home her first paycheck, her mother phoned the agency to make certain she had earned the money and not stolen it. She began to work harder, to become less insistent upon being a nurse and more realistic about her job possibilities. As her self-confidence increased, she asked for travel training. A steady, dependable worker, she missed few days and took pride in promptness. Within seven months, her attitude toward herself and others had improved markedly and vocational exploration began in earnest— evaluation for clerical work, filing, typing, switchboard, work with her hands, and the like. Helen was especially good on tasks that required fine, quick, and precise finger work, e.g. jewelry repairs.

One day, on her way to the city, Helen fell down the subway stairs. Unhurt, she returned to the program a few days later. Her courage and determination singled her out as a fighter and a winner. The accident marked the turning point for Helen and her parents. Her mother explained the change simply: "What choice did we have? We couldn't let her just sit home alone forever, could we?" But even that statement fails adequately to express the courage and faith underlying their decision. Helen had come just far enough along the road toward rehabilitation to know that she could not return to her former life of isolation. She had matured socially, was motivated to work, and had now demonstrated clearly that she could suffer setbacks yet deal constructively with them. Eventually Helen worked her way through business school studying clerical skills and typing.

Several years later, Helen and a friend revisited her old counselors and supervisors to tell about a job she had found by herself in a lettershop. She was still a shy young lady, but was more relaxed and confident. She spoke of her past and future: "Before, I was always by myself . . . and I thought I could do only low jobs, like someone without an education . . . Now I have a good job, they like me, and I am saving money in the bank."

Helen's story is a modest example of success, but it illustrates just how much more persistent handicapped youngsters must be, and how much more able to tolerate frustration and to rebound. Helen demonstrated that she could work as well as any other employee. After seizures are controlled and training and placement accomplished, the epileptic is no better or worse than other workers—neither less productive nor more accident prone. He is as ready and capable as the next fellow to do his job.

Peter

Peter's story reads like fiction but reminds us again of the extraordinary capacity people have to adjust to actual hardship. Unlike Helen, Peter responded to his medically controlled epilepsy and his home problems explosively, battling everyone and everything indiscriminately. The first question that had to be answered was could he be taught to contain his hostility until he was ready to fight creatively rather than self-destructively? Secondly, Peter's mother was suffocatingly overprotective—could they be helped to live more independently of one another?

Peter lived alone with his extremely lonely and unhappy mother who herself had a history of convulsions,
had been married three times, and had suffered five
aborted pregnancies before Peter was born. As a child,
she had borne the stigma of epilepsy and she anticipated
that Peter would suffer the same rejections and discrimination. Having learned her lesson painfully well from
society, she could hardly be blamed for accepting the
belief that an epileptic has no place in our society. In the
early years of this century, when Peter's mother was a
child, she had been placed in one of the special state
colonies established to care for epileptics. Special cus-
todial institutions and schools for epileptics existed because neither the teachers in the regular schools nor the
parents were capable of coping with their own terrified
reactions. Since those years, however, as doctors became
more knowledgeable about epilepsy, parents and teachers became more tolerant and less fearful of an occasional
seizure. There has been, therefore, a gradual decrease in
the number of outmoded custodial-oriented epileptic
colonies.

Peter had not been sent away to a special school, but
he had not been permitted to attend regular school
either. Why had he been denied the opportunity to develop emotionally, intellectually, and socially with boys
and girls his own age—especially since his seizures were
mild and infrequent? Why was he isolated from the community and made to feel unworthy and ashamed? Why
was everything done *to* rather than *for* him? The answer
is obvious: Peter's seizures did not impede his development, but the reaction of his mother and others toward
them did. When Peter was thirteen years of age, he had

been hospitalized for a few months because of severe grand mal attacks. His seizures responded so well to treatment that he rarely thereafter suffered a grand mal attack, though on occasion he experienced petit mal seizures. Despite this good fortune, his mother continued to treat him with an impending sense of doom, overwhelmed by her own memories and anxieties. Fearful and overprotective, she refused to let him out of the house alone, dreading physical harm during a seizure. No one could make her realize that she was denying her son a chance to live more normally. Understandably, such enforced segregation and confinement of a vitally energetic adolescent boy easily led to his behavioral patterns of frustration, rage, and uncontrollable behavior.

When first interviewed, Peter was, at the age of eighteen, in the tenth grade after five prior years of home instruction. He had average intellectual potential but was not working nearly as well as he could—reading on a third-grade level and doing math on a fourth-grade level. But, like Helen, he scored well enough on manual aptitude tests to suggest the advisability of further training.

Peter's mother finally agreed to his attending a work adjustment program. She demanded, however, that the agency provide transportation and prepare Peter to become a bookkeeper. This seemed unrealistic considering the low level of his reading and math skills.

A handsome, well-dressed young man, Peter at first would be naïvely charming; then, suddenly, he would grow maliciously belligerent. Alternately, Peter was depressed or angry, frightened or confused. Frustrated by his inability to understand himself, he often lost control, throwing things, screaming. His feelings of self-loathing were conspicuous; he had little insight into his problems and was poorly motivated toward improvement.

A complete account of Peter's behavior would include mention of his cooperation and his compassion toward new and timid students, along with his cruel imitations of their disabilities. He could dispense gentlemanly attention upon a young lady and follow it with cruel vulgarities. Once his endearing manner won him the almost undivided attention of a lovely blond teenager for about six months. However, the friendship came to a disastrous end, so bitter that the girl withdrew from the program.

Meanwhile, individual and group psychotherapy, vocational counseling, and regular work under supervision were beginning to produce results. Twice weekly Peter received warm, encouraging guidance directed toward helping him to behave responsibly and to cope with his mother's irrationally restrictive pattern. Clear guidelines of behavior were enforced while the relationships with staff members he trusted supported and encouraged him to discover healthier ways of relating to others.

Finally, Peter began to believe that he could take a chance on himself. He became less sullen when criticized and less despairing when he fell short of satisfactory performance of a task. His behavior with his peers improved perceptibly; bouts of exasperation diminished. Above all, his attitude toward himself altered. When he made an effort to improve his situation at home with his mother, it was clear that a significant milestone had been passed. Briefly, Peter hovered between being a "spoiled brat" at home and a responsible, contributing member of a working group. As Peter demonstrated that he could be trusted and knew how to take care of himself his mother's resistance lessened, but she still would not permit him to travel alone. Although bookkeeping lay beyond Peter's abilities (even though he raised his reading and math to sixth-grade level with remedial instruction), there was an alternative. Peter demonstrated a high potential and interest in electronic training. Until he was allowed to travel by himself, however, no such training could begin.

Finally, Peter made his own decision, aware now of what he was fighting for and what he must do to fulfill himself. In swift succession, he plotted his course through the labyrinths of both the subway and electronic training. Not too long afterward, he won an award as the student who had made most progress. Just ahead were a good job and marriage. This is not a fairy tale, however. Recently Peter visited the agency and expressed concern about an increased number of seizures. But he was neither hostile nor despairing, and he was especially pleased that his employer had been patient while his medication was being adjusted and was eager for Peter's return.

Peter and his wife had also to face the hereditary strain of epilepsy in his family. After consultation with their doctor, they determined to have the children both were eager for. They shared optimism about their own lives and hope for the future of epileptics in our society. What Peter's mother had been unable to learn from others, she learned from her son. She looked forward to becoming a grandmother.

Peter's story tells many salient facts about the rehabilitation of the epileptic. Especially noteworthy is the mother's negative and inhibiting influence. Only Peter's growing self-confidence and persistent effort eventually produced the steady faith in himself and quality of courage that made possible a happier way of life. That he managed both testifies that the epileptic is his own most convincing argument against the prejudice and ignorance of his society—and even of his family. Yet the demands placed on the sensitive are sometimes overwhelming. Parents and society must bear their burden of responsibility. When they fail, the epileptic may too.

For every Peter who has the fortitude to battle and overcome family resistance, we must realize that others have failed.

Susan

Susan is such an one. In all probability, Susan was one of the 20 percent of those epileptics unsuitable for rehabilitation outside a sheltered workshop environment. Even this could not be determined with certainty because of the formidable family interference and Susan's bewildered, angry, but passive attitude. An extremely sensitive, pretty girl, her attacks were so unusually severe that medication could not render her either seizure-free or even free of occasional side effects like drowsiness or unsteady gait. She had two or three seizures a month and on several occasions arrived with cuts and bruises suffered from falls during an attack (she had no warning before a seizure). The original lesions in her brain[12] caused grand mal seizures and considerable brain damage, which seriously impaired her behavior and her thinking. An essential point to recognize is the difference between a girl like Susan, born with intellectual potential (probably of superior level), and a person with permanently retarded abilities. Susan embodied traits and capacities of both, with flashes of superior understanding followed by periods of dull perplexity. Likewise, her scores on an intelligence test ranged from defective to high bright normal.

Susan had more than her share of trouble: her seizures resisted medical control; her academic and vocational skills were erratic and unreliable; she existed in a state of heightened uncertainty, never knowing when she might suddenly have a seizure or daring to hope for assurance of more permanence in her future. However, the crucial factor in Susan's case was her parents. From the beginning they were genuinely involved and concerned but stubbornly and blindly unrealistic. Overwhelmed by worry, harassed almost beyond endurance by Susan's misery, loneliness, and confusion, they had no reservoir of emotional or rational resources upon which they could draw for themselves or Susan. They frequently described how frantic they were every day until she safely returned home. They pressured her and her counselors for work as a bookkeeper, arguing that filing or simple office work was "beneath her." By communicating not only their panic but also their fear, and, worst of all, their unconscious shame, they sabotaged all efforts to help Susan toward a realistic acceptance of herself. Bewildered and angry, they reached out for help but were neither ready nor able to participate in the planning of a suitable rehabilitative program.

One of Susan's most distressing practices was her self-imposed silences. For a long time one suspected that she simply could not understand what was said or that perhaps she could not organize her thoughts into a sensible answer. Although both of these were sometimes the case, it was also true that with certain people Susan spoke fluently, relevantly, and intelligently. Therapy remained at a standstill until Susan eventually acknowledged that she sometimes deliberately kept silent, pretended not to understand, refused to divulge her wishes in order to anger others. But why did she want to exasperate others to the point of despair? Was it because she herself was so angry and enraged at others? Could she think of any reason she might have to be so angry? Susan stubbornly and furiously denied being angry—"at anyone or anything . . . not even my seizures!" she shrieked. After this outburst, with a sheepish smile, Susan recognized and admitted how outraged she felt. "You're right. I guess I wouldn't be shouting so loud if I really weren't so mad, huh?" But even after this admission, Susan could not participate openly and fully in therapy. She appeared regularly for her appointments, listened attentively, and seemed to benefit indirectly from the therapist's exploration of the relationship between her internal rage and fury at her seizures and the external self-defeating patterns of behavior she had developed which prevented her from making friends and from dealing more effectively with her handicap. She was furious at her parents and the whole world for not curing her of these "ugly, disgusting fits." She hated her brother because the illness had afflicted her and not him. And she hated herself for hating him but couldn't help being jealous every time he was permitted to go out alone or drive the car—"He's younger than I am and it just isn't fair!" Susan felt certain no one could ever love her, that she would never have a boy friend, get married, or have children. She was tormented by strong feelings of self-loathing, guilt, and rage and was utterly bewildered by her periodic bursts of temper. All this smoldered beneath her silence.

Although her behavior changed markedly after two years of help, she remained essentially quiet and a loner. At least she was more comfortable with herself, with adults, and with her peers in the program. Despite all the dedicated counseling and therapy Susan received, in all likelihood it was a young man—in her own words, "that good-looking boy with the blue eyes"—who influenced her most in her desire to rejoin the human race. She attended a Friday evening recreation group and began to make tentative efforts at conversation in group therapy. But both Susan and her parents have a long way to go before they reach an honest acceptance of realistic goals. The full measure of the struggle that lies ahead may be estimated by the mother's exasperated declaration to a vocational counselor when the parents applied for further business school training: "Susan doesn't have seizures. There is nothing to prevent her from becoming a secretary or bookkeeper."

Other parents, similarly motivated toward vocational rehabilitation for their child, manage nonetheless to see to it that the child fails to keep appointments for job interviews or subtly undermine his confidence and increase his self-doubt in other ways. Rarely does a parent deliberately or consciously sabotage his child's progress. For the most part, parents fail because of their own unhappiness, confusion, and helplessness.

One parent exaggerated the seriousness of her son's attacks by giving the counselor at a state rehabilitation agency the impression that he was certainly beyond all hope. In fact, the boy had occasional attacks, and those only at night, which considerably increased his chances for success in vocational training and work. The parents of Elaine, a seventeen-year-old girl, were even more destructive. Elaine was thought to be mentally defective with epilepsy, but her ability to reach a ninth-grade reading level ruled out "mental deficiency" in her diagnosis. Elaine showed excellent potential for clerical skills, but her mother insisted upon evaluation only for industrial "home" work, saying Elaine was too "stupid" for anything else, and besides, in her words, "I need Missy Eppy Lepsy to clean house. Everybody else here works." The mother not only tolerated Elaine's staying home for no apparent reason but actually encouraged absenteeism by withholding permission for her to travel. Belligerently, she undermined Elaine's hope for more autonomy. If Elaine could have managed to travel by herself, she would have been eligible at least for sheltered workshop and have earned a small amount of money—though she was certainly capable of benefiting from advanced business school training. Unhappily, Elaine remained at home, the only place her parents allowed, indeed insisted, that she could function.

The rehabilitation counselor, psychologist, social worker, and other professional personnel in the field must recognize, evaluate, and deal with the family attitude as a vitally significant part of the total picture in rehabilitating the epileptic person. It is pointless and futile to blame the parents, far better to help them understand and accept their problem candidly and realistically. Only then are they prepared to clarify their child's confusions, minimize his fears and doubts, and offer support and faith so that he can make a healthier adjustment toward a more independent and happier life.

We have learned that:

The epileptic is not retarded.
His seizures can be substantially reduced.
He is not mentally ill.
He can control and improve his behavior.
He can make friends.
He can marry and have children.
He can become an efficient, reliable worker.

To help him on his way, doctors, parents, educators, and society can and, indeed, must cooperate. As we have seen again and again, the epileptic youngster, once he has been medically stabilized, properly evaluated and trained, is for all practical purposes no longer handicapped. It is wise, of course, for him to avoid working at high altitudes or accepting work involving the use of dangerous machinery. But technically he is no more disabled because of an occasional seizure than are others who suffer from migraine, allergies, and the like.

No other physical condition has excited and stimulated social shame and scorn as has epilepsy. So great was the terror of "fits" that only repugnant explanations would do, however outlandish the false premises on which they were founded. History reminds us of the gap between knowledge and practice, but it also records the tragic waste of human life until knowledge becomes practice. In face of the failure to act upon truths that were first suggested 2,000 years ago, each truth must be rediscovered and restated until it becomes common knowledge. Only then can we expunge the errors of the past. The alternative is to place on the record another generation of victimized children.

NOTES

1. "Kondrashka" was the popular word for stroke, and "breeze" referred to the sensation Dostoevski had of a current of air just before an attack.

2. Houston Merritt and Tracy Putnam introduced Dilantin in 1937 as an anticonvulsant drug for use in control of epileptic seizures. Since then, over a dozen new anticonvulsant drugs—Mesantoin, Mysoline, Tridione, and others—have been made available for effective treatment (Kram 1963: 375).

3. At least a dozen more types of seizure have been named. Patients usually experience a mixture of two or more types of epilepsy (Goldensohn and Barrows n.d.).

4. These figures may be higher, because petit mal is frequently not as recognizable as grand mal, especially in the milder forms (Kessler 1958: 151).

5. First aid: Be calm. Do not try to restrain the person. Let him rest. Do not force anything between his teeth. Inform his parents. Do not call a doctor. (Teacher Tips n.d.).

6. Epileptic seizures may be caused by other than brain disorders, e.g. hypoglycemia, anoxia, etc. (Sands and Seaver 1966: 7–9).

7. Results of several studies of epileptic employees report that epileptics have a good attitude toward work. Their absenteeism and on-the-job accident records are better than average. There is no sub-

stantial evidence to prove any real difference between the work performances of epileptics and others (Sands and Seaver 1966: 21–26).

8. One state, West Virginia, prohibits marriage. Thirteen states authorize sterilization of epileptics under certain conditions. Ten states will not give drivers' licenses to epileptics (*Epilepsy* 1968).

9. He had, in fact, had an extremely rare form of recurrent seizures, status epileptus. Many such cases have been found to respond to medication.

10. The Board of Education usually determines when a child is sufficiently handicapped—physically or emotionally—so as not to be able to benefit from regular school attendance. In such instances a teacher is sent to the home.

11. Some rehabilitation programs secure contracts from industrial companies and can offer handicapped persons the opportunity to earn minimal wages while being vocationally evaluated.

12. Susan had an early history of Sydenham's chorea and suffered a concussion from a bicycle accident when she was ten years of age.

REFERENCES

Barrows, Howard S., and Eli S. Goldensohn, *Handbook for Parents*, New York, Ayerst Laboratories, n.d.

Epilepsy: A Survey of State Laws, Washington, D.C., Epilepsy Foundation of America, 1968.

Epilepsy: The Facts, Washington, D.C., Epilepsy Foundation of America, 1967.

Goldensohn, Eli S., and Howard S. Barrows, *Handbook for Patients*, New York, Ayerst Laboratories, n.d.

Kessler, Henry R., *Rehabilitation of the Physically Handicapped*, rev. ed., New York, Columbia University Press, 1958.

Kram, Charles, "Epilepsy in Children and Youth" in *Psychology of Exceptional Children and Youth*, 2d ed., William M. Cruickshank, ed., Englewood Cliffs, N.J., Prentice-Hall, 1963. 369–393.

Patient's Guide to Electroencephalography, A, Washington, D.C., Epilepsy Foundation of America, n.d.

Sands, Harry, and Jacqueline Seaver, *Epilepsy—Today's Encouraging Outlook*, New York, Public Affairs Committee, 1966.

Teacher Tips, Washington, D.C., Epilepsy Foundation of America, n.d.

2

Hemophilia

Hemophilia is an inherited disorder in which a vital clotting factor of the blood is lacking. In its most serious form, hemophilia—which mostly affects males[1]—strikes as many people in this country as polio struck before the Salk vaccine became available. Recognized and documented in early Talmudic writings, hemophilia became a "disease of kings" when Queen Victoria transmitted it to ten or twelve male descendants. To suffer a "royal disease" gave little comfort to tens of thousands of "bleeders" who lived in the shadow of the prevailing diagnosis and prognosis: a rare, incurable disease whose victims rarely survive to adulthood. There is still no cure for hemophilia, but since 1960, there has been real cause for optimism. Though the disorder is not yet curable, *it can now be controlled.* During the 1960's, significant discoveries in hematology laboratories have brought new hope of prolonged life to some 100,000 American hemophiliacs, and have compelled writers of medical dictionaries to revise and update the facts about hemophilia.

A hemophiliac bears many burdens—emotional, economical, educational, social, and vocational. But his primary need is for expert medical care. To be a hemophiliac means living each day in fear of hemorrhage— not, as is popularly thought, uncontrollable bleeding from a small cut, but dangerous internal bleeding and bleeding into the joints. Severe internal hemorrhage may be accompanied by fever, swelling, muscle contractions, and pain, as well as by the possibility of serious and permanent deformity of arms and legs. Thus, the hemophiliac must avail himself of the most modern techniques of hemorrhage control. Hemorrhage control not only saves life, but also helps to avoid shock and anemia and to prevent damage to joints, vital organs, nerves, and muscles.

The two most common varieties of inherited bleeding disorders are hemophilia A, known as classic hemophilia, with Factor VIII deficiency;[2] and hemophilia B, or Christmas Disease, with Factor IX deficiency. Six times as many patients suffer with hemophilia A as with hemophilia B. Together they represent about 85 percent of all persons with inherited coagulation disorders.[3] Both types are inherited through an abnormal sex-linked gene and have similar symptoms, but they must be distinguished from one another for purposes of treatment. (Strauss 1967: 1).

Further categories are useful in describing the intensity of the disease itself, namely, severe, moderately severe, and mild deficiency (Strauss 1967:.6). Knowing both the specific type and severity of illness is crucial to effective diagnosis and treatment. Other data are also necessary: a detailed past history of bleeding events, an exhaustive family history, and laboratory test results.[4] Only after a thorough examination can a physician initiate the therapeutic program of treatment most suitable for a specific bleeding disorder.[5] Otherwise minor accidents may become major struggles for survival. Years ago, for example, a tooth extraction required transfusions of from 10 to 100 pints of blood (in rare instances as many as 200 or 300) and more serious operations often needed 1,000 transfusions (*World Journal Tribune* 1967: B5). An appendectomy required months in the hospital and large and expensive quantities of blood. Many minor operations were never performed because of the risk to life.

For many years, the treatment for patients suffering from bleeding episodes was transfusions of fresh whole blood. Throughout this period, doctors tried to learn why transfusions sometimes helped to control bleeding. Their research showed that the clotting time for hemophiliacs is prolonged but that the bleeding time is normal. However, no really satisfactory explanation appeared until 1935, when the basic defect in hemophilia— a clotting deficiency—became generally known. Doctors reasoned that transfusions worked because the new blood contained small amounts of the deficient clotting agent. Once the cause was clear, the need for improved treatment was equally apparent. The volume of whole blood needed to supply the missing factor was too great; moreover, transfusions took too long to administer at safe intervals. Always there was the risk that the patient's heart or other vital organs might become overworked. Or further, if too much time elapsed before the bleeding could be stopped, crippling damage to joints would occur.

Understandably, the goal in research for years has been, first, to extract the clotting agent from whole blood and, second, to concentrate it for speedier and more effective control of hemorrhage. By 1940, Dr. K. Brinkhous (along with many other dedicated doctors) had demonstrated the presence of Factor VIII in plasma (the clear liquid portion of blood). Plasma transfusions had become the treatment of choice since plasma eliminated the threat of transfusing too many red cells, did not have to be typed, and could be frozen and stored. But volume remained a critical problem. By 1965, a major breakthrough was made with the discovery by Dr. Judith Pool, and others, of the first concentrate—cryoprecipitate, which was ten to twenty times stronger than plasma. Three and one half ounces of the new preparation had the potency of ten pints of blood. Cryoprecipitate quickly became standard treatment, but only for use with hemophilia A, Factor VIII deficiency. Accounts of near-miracle results were reported across the country. By 1968, methods of extracting the AHF factor were improved upon, and its potency was increased thirty to fifty times over plasma (more recent concentrates have been reported to be even more potent) ("Help for Hemophiliacs" 1968: 66). As techniques grow more efficient and concentrates are purified, there may be fewer allergic reactions.

It is extremely important to remember, however, that if the particular type of hemophilia has not been diagnosed, only fresh whole blood or fresh plasma can be used. Effective concentrates have been developed for use with laboratory-verified hemophilia A and B patients. Hemophilia A is treated with concentrates for major hemorrhage, whereas hemophilia B can be treated safely with banked plasma for both minor and major hemorrhage. Concentrates are being developed for other less common deficiencies (Factor X) as well (Strauss 1967: 24–28).

It is readily apparent, then, that today's doctors have more knowledge of hemophilia as a disease and are far better equipped to treat and control its symptoms. Today a ruptured appendix may be successfully operated upon, and the patient released after no more than three weeks in the hospital. Tooth extractions are safe and may be performed expeditiously. Even major surgery, when indicated, may be faced with confidence. Other advantages have also become available. For instance, the new concentrates can occasionally be used preventively. Some hemophiliacs can receive hypodermic injections in the doctor's office within five minutes after an episode of bleeding. It is anticipated that others may soon be able to inject themselves, as diabetics use insulin (*New York Times* 1968: 7). Late in 1970 doctors reported that successful procedures had been developed for home injection of the clotting factor—an important advance in treating hemorrhage as soon as it occurs.

Techniques in orthopedic and physical therapy have joined with blood research in the battle to prevent and to correct crippling effects of hemophilia. In many instances where joints have already been damaged, orthopedic treatment and the use of braces have restored the patient to nearly normal functioning and permitted him to follow a sensible schedule at school or work.

One aspect of hemophilia—its hereditary pattern—requires special consideration. Hemophilia affects mostly males, as we have seen, whereas only females (all the daughters and about half the sisters) can pass the disease on, or are "carriers" of the abnormal, sex-linked gene (Lewis 1966). Many hemophiliacs fail to understand that their sons cannot inherit their illness: all their sons will be normal. But all their daughters will be carriers. Thus, hemophilia always skips at least one generation and, since it is impossible to predict how many of the sons of a carrier will inherit the disease (or even how many of her daughters will become carriers)[6] conceivably several generations may pass with no outcropping of hemophilia. Such families are not uncommon. Neither, however, are cases of hemophilia where there has been no family history of hemophilia whatsoever. As the search continues for deeper insight into the transmission of hemophilia, the role of the genetic counselor in family planning has become increasingly important.

Psychological implications for the hemophiliac and his family are predictably abundant. A mother weeps with grief and guilt. *She* carried the ill-fated gene. She feels responsible for her son's misery, his suffering, and for the mounting bills. Overwhelmed by remorse, convinced that she is at fault, she strives to protect, but more often succeeds only in overprotecting. Consequently, the likelihood of achieving her goal—to raise a hemophiliac son who can live as normal and independent a life as possible—is considerably diminished. Every mother wishes her son to possess self-confidence and an assurance that he can meet life's experiences responsibly, but many mothers fail to see incompatibility between their goal and their practice. Mothers of hemophiliacs are especially vulnerable, and their sons are often treated as if, like the disease, they are "royal." It is scarcely surprising that psychiatric studies of hemophilic teenagers should indicate that many of their psychic problems derive from the intensity of their relationship with an overprotective mother (Agle and Mattson n.d.: 2).

The hemophilic child's relationship with his parents is often the determinant in a satisfactory, realistic adjustment or an inadequate compromise. Much depends upon the father's reaction. If he accepts and shares responsibility for the care and upbringing of his son, he may reduce the mother's overwhelming sense of guilt and not deprive the boy of the masculine image he needs. Moreover, if the father is sincerely involved with his boy's welfare, he may compensate for the mother's excesses by encouraging healthy, aggressive sports rather than a frightened, passive retreat. After her son has undergone numerous emergency transfusions and lengthy, painful, and expensive hospitalizations, a misguided mother may reason that the only way to prevent mishaps is to prohibit *all* activities. True, the boy must avoid falls and he dare not engage in rough-and-tumble games. Even playful jostling may result in ambulance calls and hours of anguish. But both mother and son err when they fail to discriminate between an excessive proscription of activities and a reasonable range as prescribed by the doctor. Likewise, they fail to recognize and accept that bleeding may occur despite the most rigid restrictions. To be sure, it is a fine line and there is no guarantee that on either side lies total freedom from future bleeding episodes. One thing is certain, however. Unless the mother, as well as all other responsible adults in the family, determines upon a course of sensible precautions and adheres to otherwise sound principles of child upbringing, her son cannot be expected to develop into an emotionally stable, independent individual.

All too quickly, otherwise, the boy may sense an "advantage" in his fragility and depend upon his mother and others to fulfill every wish and need. Or, conversely, deprived of the opportunity to understand and control his own behavior, to live as normally as is possible, he may turn belligerent and rebel against his mother's restrictions. The pattern is common among hemophiliacs —and most unfortunate. Some adolescent hemophiliacs whose mothers are overprotective seem deliberately to engage in risky activities. It is misleading to speak of the hemophiliac as "accident-prone." Rather, it is as if he baldly denies his illness and foolhardily courts disaster by repeatedly testing his vulnerability. Apart from the physical dangers, such rebellion generates tension and emotional strain. Although no definitive cause-and-effect relationship has been demonstrated between emotional stress and increased bleeding episodes, the two are undeniably commonplace among hemophilic patients (Didisheim 1966; Agle and Mattson n.d.: 4).

Other reactions that may be anticipated because of frequent bleeding, physical pain, and repeated separations from their family are strong feelings of being different, and therefore inferior. The threat of immobility is very real for some patients who have endured days or weeks in a cast intended to prevent permanent crippling to their joints and limbs. Some youngsters expend undue amounts of mental and physical energy on neurotic defense activities and pay dearly in the sum of their intellectual and emotional well-being. Some live in terror of being abandoned by one or both of their parents, and others sink apathetically into helpless depression or cling to immature behavior, neither participating in nor benefiting from rehabilitative programs.

There are, however, healthier, more gratifying ways than those mentioned above of learning to live with hemophilia. Those hemophiliacs and their families who have made more successful and realistic accommodations to the illness have managed to do so by accepting the limitations of the disability and avoiding overreactions of dependence or revolt. The hemophiliac is, first, a boy who needs tutoring in the ways of becoming a man. He needs a sense of his own worth, belief in his ability to work and achieve, and respect for independent effort. He is also a boy who must compete for and achieve these goals within the context of specifically defined activities. As the child grows up, he should be taught everything there is to know about his condition, including realistic precautions and what he must do in case of accident. Rather than permit fear, withdrawal, or passivity, he must be encouraged to participate fully in acceptable peer activities at school and play. Depending upon the severity of his hemophilia, he may engage in such sports as golf, tennis, swimming, archery, and boating, as well as in more sedentary interests such as chess, stamp collecting, building models, reading, or other pastimes related to his interests. It is common therapeutic knowledge that healthy physical activity helps to reduce anxiety and emotional stress. Little wonder, then, that some clinical findings suggest fewer hemorrhages among physically active hemophiliacs. It is also noteworthy that even with some hemophiliacs who at first had sought refuge in passivity and later learned to compete more aggressively, the frequency of bleeding episodes diminished. What, then, should the parents do for their son? Within the special limits imposed by the disease, they should behave with very little difference from any other parents. Enduring misfortune may explain but cannot justify departure from common-sense practice.

Taking care of one's teeth is routine for normal youngsters; for the hemophiliac it is a matter of special concern. The hemophilic boy must take meticulous care of his teeth, not because they are structurally inferior (Rubin and Levine 1966), but because of the need to avoid the prolonged bleeding that follows extractions. If preventive measures are followed, including attention to oral hygiene, diet, and frequent visits to the dentist, there should be little need for emergency treatment. Undoubtedly, many hemophiliacs recall varied difficulties after a tooth extraction: prolonged stays in the hospital; clumsy, painful techniques to stop oral bleeding; transfusions, anemia, fatigue, loss of weight, and, as always, absence from home, school, or work.

A letter written by Tommy, a hemophilic teenager, illustrates a dramatically different kind of dental experience: "Dear Friends, Thanks for your get-well card, but hear this—it had to be forwarded to my home from the hospital because I was discharged in a couple of days! I was scared stiff at first by all the tests and preparations they made before they pulled my tooth, and because I remembered what happened three years ago. But was I surprised! Tell Bobby I needed only one transfusion!"

Tommy had better not stop brushing his teeth. And he cannot have all the candy, sweets, and soda pop he wants. Neither can he avoid regular and frequent visits to the dentist. As a child, before he was old enough to realize the risk, he recalled lying about having brushed his teeth, and refusing to eat any but soft, mushy foods so as to avoid irritating his gums. By the time he was ten, however, a bad toothache and infection required surgery. Tommy spent six weeks away from home and school. Those memories, as well as the dentist's patient and skillful corrective and restorative treatment, gave Tommy reason enough thereafter to practice sensible preventive habits. Happily, methods of extraction and dental care for hemophiliacs have improved dramatically (Rubin, Levine, and Rosenthal 1959). Though advances have been made, reasonable precautions must always be taken and oral surgery should be performed at a hospital.

Kenneth

At home and at school there are also a number of safety precautions that should be taken (*The Hemophiliac and His School* n.d.: 1–5). The hemophilic boy and his family need to prepare and prevent. They need always to be alert in order to avoid injury. The reckless regret.

When Kenneth transferred to a new high school, his adjustment was facilitated by a visit his parents made to the school. They advised the school physician that

Kenneth had severe hemophilia (classic) and noted his blood type for the school's records. They volunteered to have Kenneth's doctor provide a full history of his past illness and to recommend limits to Kenneth's activities. (Following the doctor's advice—that too many prohibitions were likely to be as harmful as too few—Kenneth had already learned to swim, play tennis, enjoy chess, and he was an enthusiastic baseball fan.) Gym activities would be carefully monitored. Although Kenneth was permitted to use public transportation, he was cautioned not to climb stairs with crowds of students. Therefore, he was given an elevator pass. The school even offered to provide Kenneth with an extra set of books to be kept at home, eliminating the need to carry books back and forth.

Furthermore, the principal agreed that Kenneth's attendance in regular classes would serve his best interests. He had suffered no particular learning difficulties as a function of hemophilia and he needed no teachers with any special training. His parents were especially eager to enlist the understanding and cooperation of his teachers in treating Kenneth as a normal boy in all respects—intellectual, emotional, and social—other than his hemophilic needs. And about his hemophilia, they resolved to protect but not to overprotect. Kenneth's teachers agreed to provide his classmates with information about hemophilia in order to prevent as many careless accidents as possible and to avoid Kenneth's being branded as "different." Fortunately, the teaching staff was sensitive to the influence their attitudes might have toward Kenneth's adjustment and acceptance of his condition.

In spite of all these thoughtful precautions, the inevi-

table happened—one day Kenneth was unavoidably jos-
tled in a crowded elevator. He was thrown to the floor
and his left arm painfully twisted. School officials immediately notified his parents and their doctor. In the
meantime, Kenneth wasted no time applying basic first
aid measures. He lay down in the nurse's office to rest,
holding his left arm as still as possible. After the application of cold, wet compresses to relieve the pain and
reduce possible swelling, he assured his friends and
teachers that he could wait until he arrived home to
apply an elastic bandage or perhaps a splint that would
further immobilize his arm. On other occasions—a nose
bleed and a minor cut—Kenneth's advice to apply a
coagulant preparation with firm pressure had worked
fine.[7]

This time Kenneth was not so lucky. By nightfall
(after a visit to his doctor) it was evident that internal
bleeding had started in his left knee as well as in his
elbow and shoulder. He received a transfusion and the
doctor suggested that he rest at home. A few years earlier, fear and panic would have spread from Kenneth to
his parents. Now, however, a matter-of-fact attitude
prevailed. Arrangements had already been made at
school (in case of prolonged absence) to provide a qualified teacher for home instruction. Thus, Kenneth re-
tained both his interest in learning and his grade level.
Previously, he had dropped behind in his studies, become bored, apathetic, and depressed. Such understanding, cooperation, and support among patient,
family, physician, and school authorities are rare but
highly desirable. Doubtless the smooth passage of Kenneth's high school years was closely related to the

thoughtful planning and cooperation of all involved personnel.

Vocational counseling also played a role in Kenneth's school curriculum. And so it should have, since it is especially important for hemophiliacs (indeed, for all handicapped persons) to face a prejudiced job market fully prepared—even overprepared—to compete for the job of their choice. Vocational counselors must be practical and realistic, guiding hemophiliacs toward areas where their services may be needed, yet avoiding occupations that demand excessive physical exertion (Katz 1963: 1673–74).

Kenneth benefited from wise vocational counseling. Not until his senior year in high school would he abandon his boyhood dream to become a surgeon and acknowledge that his skills in math and science were inadequate. Almost with a sense of relief, he agreed that the prospect of four years in a liberal arts college, to be followed, possibly, by law school, sounded "just great."

Jimmie

Kenneth's experiences, of course, are not always duplicated. Jimmie had hemophilia too—of moderately severe deficiency. Unlike Kenneth, he simply had not learned how to live sensibly or realistically with his illness. When Jimmie was nineteen, he (and his parents) boasted about his physical activities to a vocational counselor in an engineering college. "The doctor said I'm just like any other normal kid. No difference." Ever-so-slightly bending advice to suit their purpose, Jimmie and his parents failed to set the firm guidelines needed to adjust to the fact of the boy's illness. Experience suggests that while patients may not outgrow the disease, the condition sometimes becomes more stable with age because the patient learns to accept responsibility for his own well-being. Not so with Jimmie. Although his was among the less serious of hemophilic conditions, he required frequent and prolonged periods of hospitalization. Once recovered, he began immediately to take new risks—drag-racing his car, taking long hikes, and dancing for many hours—all activities courting bruises, sprains, and bleeding.

Jimmie and his parents behaved as though they had tacitly conspired to avoid an honest confrontation of Jimmie's disorder and to evade any awareness of how their denial affected his actions or vocational plans for the future. Obligingly, Jimmie acted out his role. When the guidance counselor suggested that Jimmie curtail some of his vigorous activities, he responded, "What's wrong with having a good time? It's only natural for fellas my age, isn't it?" He ignored the seriousness of his disability or the need for physical restrictions. Again, when he and his counselor were discussing his low grades (despite his more than adequate intellectual ability) and the very real possibility that he would not be permitted to register next semester, Jimmie could not deal frankly with himself or the reality of failing. Instead, he offered the lame cliché "All kids hate to study, don't they? I guess I'm just lazy, but I'll hit the books from now on, really I will."

The charade continued at home. His mother masked her guilt by indulging Jimmie's irresponsibility; his father harangued about spoiling the boy. Neither helped him toward responsible independence. Instead, he grew ever less able to cope with his deep sense of personal inadequacy. Beneath the bravado lay an obsessive fear of imminent death, a fear that might have been diminished had Jimmie—and his parents—been able to accept the fact of a moderately severe hemophilia whose prognosis reads "excellent control, with proper care and treatment."

There are as many ways to live with hemophilia as there are hemophiliacs. Each person may exaggerate an aspect of his response to school, self, parents, or work. At eighteen, Harold clung dependently and immaturely to his boyish ways, resisting doctor's advice to learn to walk with crutches and to get out of his wheelchair. Too frightened to accept the challenge to plan for his vocational future, he refused advanced training, even though he showed aptitude for both accounting and computer programming.

Richard, whose father had left home when he was an infant, suffered a deficiency as mild as his depression was severe. His gloom yielded gradually after months of therapy patiently hammered at simple clarification of facts: he *could* consider marriage; he could *not* transmit his disease to future sons; he was capable of work and showed a potential for electronic training or jewelry work. All he needed was further training and special job placement. The family, doctor, and teachers of a hemophilic child should strive for a good working balance between realistic precautions and an equally realistic occupation for the future.

No account of hemophilia can end without reference

to Dr. Murray Thelin (Deutsch and Deutsch 1967: 40), himself a hemophiliac, whose life, though fraught with pain and frustration, was enriched by courage and perseverance. Determined to contribute toward making life safer and longer for future hemophiliacs, he specialized in blood chemistry when he was denied acceptance for medical training. Together with Drs. Brinkhous, Wagner, Pool, Shanbrom, and others, he dedicated his life to perfecting concentrates. He labored under conditions detrimental to his own health, and when at last in 1966, he neared success, he died. But not before he had dramatically proved, using himself as his own guinea pig, that his newly prepared powdered concentrate worked almost miraculously. When he suffered a brain hemorrhage, he ordered the use of his own concentrate. The bleeding stopped and he was out of the hospital in ten days. Moreover, he demonstrated that the new preparation could be used safely as a preventive. A regimen of weekly injections freed him from even a single bleeding, even after he was injured in an auto crash. At a later date, when injections were deliberately withheld, he began again to bleed, hemorrhaging at the slightest provocation.

Ironically, progress often creates new problems. It is estimated that hemophiliacs need the AFH factor from one million pints of blood every year. Not nearly enough pints are donated. Supplies are short and expensive. Means must be found to reduce the exorbitant financial burden—estimated as between $4,000 to $6,000 annually—upon the hemophiliac and his family. Finally, as innovations have enabled hemophiliacs to live longer, marry, and have children, the number of hemophiliacs needing

blood, treatment, and money for such care has also increased. If more hemophiliacs are to live the longer,
more normal life that has now been made possible for
them, research must press forward and society must find
ways to meet the expense involved.

NOTES

1. A small number of females have evidenced atypical bleeding
problems. However, they remain the exception to the rule.

2. Other terms referring to Factor VIII deficiency are AHF, AHG,
antihemophilic factor, and globulin AHG.

3. Other inherited clotting deficiencies make up the remaining 15
percent and include hemophilia C, lacking Factor XI, von Willen-
brand's disease—often called pseudo-hemophilia—platelet dysfunc-
tions, and other relatively rare inherited coagulation disorders.

4. Glass clotting time and bleeding times are of no value when used
by themselves. Recommended procedures, after recording personal
and family history: (1) observation of whole blood for clot activity, (2)
Quick's prothrombin time, (3) partial thromboplastin time, (4) Bleeding time (Ivy Method) and (5) Wright stained smear of peripheral
blood for evaluation of platelets.

5. For instance, only certain of the new medical preparations
(known as concentrates) may be used for hemophilia A. Furthermore,
the choice of blood products and method of treatment are indicated
by the kind of bleeding (internal soft tissue bleeding or surface
wound bleeding). Dosage must be calculated according to the severity
of the deficiency, the patient's size, and the potency of the product.
If hemophilia has been diagnosed as severe, the physician may expect
spontaneous hemorrhage into muscle, knees, or elbows, but with
moderately severe or mild hemophilia, he may expect hemorrhages
to occur less frequently and as a result of injury or surgery. In either
case he may determine the most suitable method of treatment with
the most effective blood product available.

6. It is believed that about half the sons of a carrier inherit hemophilia and half her daughters become carriers.

7. Items that should be on hand at all times: elastic bandages, Hot-R-Cold Paks, ice bags and ice throat collars, foam rubber, adhesive tape, Band-Aids, orangewood sticks, absorbent cotton, gauze, coagulants, Methocel, Thrombin-loco' or 5,000-unit vials, adrenalin, Gelfoam, Oxycel gauze or HemoPak, medications prescribed by doctor, mineral oil and cotton rolls.

REFERENCES

Agle, David P., and A. Mattson, *Emotional Health in Hemophilia*, New York, National Hemophilia Foundation, n.d.

Deutsch, Patricia, and Ron Deutsch, "One Man's Fight Against Hemophilia," *Today's Health* 45 (1967): 40–43.

Didisheim, Paul, "Mechanism of Bleeding and Hemostasis in the Hemophilias," *Hemophilia vol. 1, no. 1*, 1966.

"Help for Hemophiliacs," *Time*, August 16, 1968.

Hemophiliac and His School, The, New York, National Hemophilia Foundation, n.d.

Katz, Alfred H., "Social Adaptation in Chronic Illness: A Study of Hemophilia," *American Journal of Public Health and the Nation's Health* 53 (1963): 1660–75.

Lewis, Jessica H., "The Inheritance of Hemophilia," *Hemophilia vol. 1, no. 1*, 1966.

New York Times, Sept. 8, 1968, Section IV, p. 7, col. 1.

Rubin, Benjamin, and Paul Levine, *Care and Treatment of Teeth of Hemophiliacs*, New York, National Hemophilia Foundation, 1966.

Rubin, Benjamin, Paul Levine, and Martin C. Rosenthal, "Complete Dental Care of the Hemophiliac," *Oral Surgery, Oral Medicine, and Oral Pathology 12, no. 6* (1959): 665–75.

Strauss, Herbert S., *Diagnosis and Treatment of Hemophilia*, Boston, Children's Hospital Medical Center, 1967.

World Journal Tribune, New York, April 23, 1967, B5.

3

Sickle Cell Anemia

Sickle cell anemia is another inherited, noncontagious, incurable blood disorder about which very little is understood. The most startling facts about this illness are the large numbers of those afflicted and the pervasive public ignorance about the disease. Even among the black population, which suffers almost alone the full impact of this dread disability, most have never heard of sickle cell anemia. They do not know what it is, how simply it may be detected, and how critically it affects one out of four hundred black Americans. Inconclusive statistics report that sickle cell anemia has stricken between 45,000 and 600,000 Americans. Approximately another thousand infants are born annually with the disease.

Until very recently, the chances of living a full normal life span—if the patient survived childhood—were slim. But many changes are taking place as new organizations publicize the disease and launch campaigns to raise money for medical research. At last, misinformation about sickle cell anemia is being corrected and a concentrated effort is being made to use what has long been known but never applied in the treatment of innumerable undiagnosed and neglected cases. Improved, easily administered tests have been devised—all of them suitable for mass screening of sickle cell anemia. Healthy controversy reigns over periodic claims of a "breakthrough" in treatment. Local communities have begun to sponsor mass screening and educational programs. And, most important, the federal government has increased its allotment for sickle cell anemia research and treatment to $6 million, and current legislation should provide $25 million annually for the next three years toward additional treatment centers whose services will include genetic counseling and follow-up examinations ("Now Eddie Smith . . . " 1971).

At one time it was thought that black people alone inherited sickle cell anemia; whites inherited a similar blood disorder, thalassemia. Today, medicine knows that anyone—of whatever color—of African origin may transmit sickle cell anemia. A curious irony attended its inception since the sickle cell trait (a *single* inherited sickle cell gene) functions as protection against malaria. As a rule, millions without the sickle cell trait died of the fever; those with the trait developed a stronger survival strain of the cell and passed it on to their offspring. Now that malaria can be controlled, the trait is largely useless, but the double dose of genes—the full anemic disease—is destructive and potentially fatal for thousands of its victims.

Ignorance about this disease is even more remarkable when one considers that there are more people who have sickle cell anemia than there are those who suffer such highly publicized disorders as muscular dystrophy, hemophilia, cystic fibrosis, childhood leukemia or phenylketonuria (PKU).[1] In cities that have a black population of 30 percent, it is estimated that more than twice as many black children are born with sickle cell anemia as white children with cystic fibrosis, and nearly nine times as many as those with PKU (Scott 1970b). Still, in 1968, only $50,000 was raised to fight sickle cell anemia, whereas muscular dystrophy received more than $7 million dollars for medical research. Some doctors regard sickle cell anemia as the most neglected health problem in our society. Clearly, much more progress needs to be made in research, education, prevention, and health care.

It was not until 1922 that the disease was named sickle cell anemia (SCA), although the first reported case had appeared in medical journals ten years earlier. The defect was located in the red blood cells and, in 1949, Dr. Linus Pauling, the distinguished chemist, discovered the "abnormal hemoglobin molecule that causes red blood cells to sickle," that is, to twist into the shape of a sickle. In this form of anemia, hemoglobin—the protein substance in the red blood cells, which distribute oxygen to all parts of the body—has an irregular molecular structure. Pauling perfected the technique, known as electro-

phoresis, that pinpointed the irregularity in the hemoglobin of the red blood cells. Pauling's achievement her-
alded the new discipline of molecular biology and
pointed up its relationship to medicine. Dr. V. M. In-
gram in England further demonstrated the substitution
of one amino acid for another in the hemoglobin of sickle
cell anemia victims. Much of what is known about SCA
has been discovered, then, during the past fifty or sixty
years. But understanding the mechanism that results in
sickle cell anemia has not produced effective prevention,
treatment, or cure.

In their altered form, the sickled blood cells are fragile
and have less chance than normal cells to survive. Frequently, they cannot flow through the smaller arteries.
They cluster together, pile up or "clump," and form
blood clots, which impede the normal flow of blood to
local tissues. The more rapid destruction of these sickled
cells and the decreased amount of oxygen transported
increase the likelihood of infection and damage to other
organs of the body. The external symptoms are general
weakness and listlessness. In more severe cases—termed
"sickle cell crises"—the symptoms vary from anemia,
headaches, and jaundice to nausea, vomiting, fever, and
swelling. Some patients endure repeated episodes of
severe pains in muscles, limbs, chest, joints, stomach,
and back. Leg ulcers, dizziness, ringing in the ears, and
spots before the eyes are other likely symptoms. At
times, patients may become drowsy, irritable, or belligerent. Or, as with other severe anemias, the victims may
be poorly developed physically—short trunks, long arms
and legs; barrel-shaped chests and protruding abdomens.

Sometimes, diagnosis is difficult because of the

similarity between the symptoms of sickle cell anemia
and those of rheumatic fever and other abdominal nerve
disorders (U.S. Dept. of H., E., and W. n.d.). Even
though blood tests can determine whether the red blood
cells are sickling, without additional symptoms the condition cannot be diagnosed as sickle cell anemia. Instead,
the patient is said to be a "carrier" of the sickle cell trait.
A carrier is a person who receives one imperfect gene
from one of his parents. Only when a child inherits two
sickle cell genes, one from each parent, does he suffer the
full effect of sickle cell anemia. The probability is that
one out of four children born of parents each of whom
has the sickle cell trait will inherit sickle cell anemia; two
out of four may be carriers, and one out of four may
escape both the disease and the trait. Dr. Scott estimates
that one out of 144 families runs the risk of both parents
carrying the trait. Black parents should insist upon
blood tests for all of their children so that carriers of the
trait may be identified. This step is crucial for saving life
and for future family planning.

Why is it so important to identify persons with the
sickle cell trait, a task, incidentally, which is very easily
accomplished by simple blood tests (Uslick 1970)? Because, for hundreds of thousands of people it may mean,
as we shall see shortly, the difference between a tragic,
shortened lifetime of illness and a relatively normal life
span free of pain. It is calculated that among the two
million (one out of ten) American blacks who are carriers
(those who have inherited the sickle cell trait) the great
majority are totally unaware that some of their red blood
cells are sickle-shaped instead of round. Furthermore,
they are ignorant of the grave consequences this may

have upon their own future and their children's—
whether they will enjoy normal healthy lives or be
plagued with periodic bouts of pain, perpetual need for
medical care, and forced to live within highly restricted
patterns of activity.

Although a carrier may be free of all symptoms except
the presence of the sickled red blood cell in his blood,
under certain conditions his otherwise benign condition
can become activated and result in either sudden death
or a lifetime of suffering. It is inconceivable that everyone in the black community has not been screened for
the sickle cell trait and advised of the existing dangers to
his life. For instance, all activities that would normally
reduce the oxygen content to the body should be cur-
tailed or eliminated. Alcoholic beverages must be avoided, swimming under water is dangerous, physical exercise in high altitudes is prohibited, and the use of
anesthesia may be counterindicated. Yet only in recent
years have a few doctors begun routinely to test for the
sickle cell trait before surgery, and also to ask for blood
tests before approving participation in organized sports,
or induction into the Army (the Air Force automatically
tests for sickle cell trait).

No known medical cure exists for sickle cell anemia,
but many of the symptoms can be treated and complications prevented. Pain-killing drugs are used. Ice packs
applied to joints inhibit "clumping" of the twisted cells
and facilitate circulation of the blood. Blood transfusions
and bed rest alleviate acute, painful attacks. Perhaps
most significant, since the discovery of antibiotics, infections have been kept to a minimum. Whereas most patients with sickle cell anemia formerly died at an early

age, or rarely survived beyond their fortieth year, today
their life span has been substantially extended.

Time magazine ("Discriminating . . ." 1970; "Detecting
. . ." 1971), *Drug Therapy* (Nalbandian 1971), and the *Journal
of the American Medical Association* ("New Strategy . . ."
1971) have all reported a new approach to treatment for
sickle cell anemia that offers relief from suffering and
renewed hope for a cure. Dr. Robert Nalbandian, of
Blodgett Memorial Hospital in Grand Rapids, pursued
Makio Murayama's hypothesis "that the sickle-cell shape
is caused by abnormal bonding between hemoglobin
molecules in the red cells" (Nalbandian *et al.* 1971). Despite claims that experiments have demonstrated that
urea in invert sugar has effected—without unpleasant
consequences—unsickling of cells, restored circulation,
and has dramatically relieved pain, many doctors believe
that the evidence is inconclusive. Critics acknowledge
Dr. Nalbandian's significant contributions: he has increased public interest and spurred involvement; he has
improved and rendered more "specific" automated
screening tests for sickle cell anemia; he has encouraged
the use of mass screening and educational community
programs; and, of course, he has offered new methods of
treatment. However, Dr. Lemuel Diggs (to cite but one
skeptic) urges more restraint about accepting claims of
successful treatment and cure of sickle cell crises by use
of urea (Diggs 1971). The form of intravenous therapy
whereby urea in an invert sugar solution is injected into
the superior vena cava, for example, requires highly
skilled personnel and costly intensive care facilities, including ongoing chemical and hematological monitoring. Furthermore, since sickle cell anemia itself varies

considerably in severity and response to different methods of treatment, it is not at all certain that the results noted were due only to the use of urea.

Urea is a natural waste product, part of normal urine, which can be readily and inexpensively synthesized in the laboratory. Its value in the fight against sickling red blood cells is that it can easily pass through cell membranes, break up molecular bonds, and allow the altered hemoglobin to revert to its soluble state. Of course, if treatment is not begun before obstruction by sickled, clumped cells, urea or any other form of treatment is seriously hampered. Finally, Dr. Diggs reminds us that urea can also cause other molecular alterations not directly related to sickle cell hemoglobin.

Other substances are also being tested. At Rockefeller University Dr. James Manning and others claim that cyanate is more efficient and less dangerous than urea in its protection against sickling. What is most encouraging is that scientists everywhere are at last engaged in massive research into SCA. Special SCA clinics are being opened where not only testing and treatment are offered, but where followup examinations and critical genetic counseling—the most reliable preventive measure extant —is available (Scott 1970a).

Howard

Some patients manage, despite chronic pain and weakness, to cope with a normal amount of daily activity. Not so with Howard, a sullen seventeen-year-old who complained excessively, blamed others (especially his family) for all his problems, and at school ducked all responsibility for attendance and punctuality, as well as the need to cooperate or participate in school assignments. Later, in a rehabilitation program, he showed little motivation to change.

None of the more severe symptoms of sickle cell anemia were present daily, but since the age of ten, when his condition was first diagnosed, Howard had had frequent attacks of stomach pains (with or without medication) and frequent periods of hospitalization during which he received blood transfusions and medication for pain. Howard and his family did not believe that he was seriously ill. But the records clearly indicated a need for family consultation. When interviewed by a social worker, Howard's father vehemently denied having any trouble with his son at home. "He's a good boy, always obeys me, has lots of friends, and gets along okay with his brothers and sisters. His only problem is that he gets tired easily." His mother, on the other hand, badgered Howard about being lazy, told him he was no good and would never be able to work. His brother seemed to understand Howard better, saying, "He does have bad pains sometimes but he builds them up to goof off. He can be real trouble when he wants to be—real evil."

Howard was nervous, tense, depressed a good deal of the time, and always enraged with anyone who did not agree with him immediately when he argued "My family don't like me and always pick on me." His behavior was so objectionable and his manner so unpleasant that all efforts failed to help him work out some of his rebelliousness at home or elsewhere. Equally unavailing were attempts to deal more reasonably with his illness, for Howard refused to follow medical advice, drank inordinate amounts of Bromo-Seltzer and Pepto-Bismol for "my stomach aches," played baseball too strenuously, and rested very little. Indeed, he seemed to be courting an early death by denying that there was anything wrong with him at all. Everyone behaved as though Howard just did not have sickle cell anemia and did not go to the hospital at least four or five times a year. Even his teacher reported that Howard was "lazy and unreliable as a student and his pains are of emotional origin." Howard's gloom persisted, his complaints about his family continued, and his pains went unabated. At eighteen, Howard was dead.

Harriet

Occasionally shame is added to the sense of bewilderment that many victims of sickle cell anemia experience. For a long time, no one could fathom the reasons for Harriet's refusal to keep appointments for vocational counseling or therapy. She was an unusually bright, sensible, and attractive young girl of seventeen with a variety of vocational alternatives at her disposal—community college, key-punch operator, or secretarial work. Friendly, pleasant, and cooperative, she related well to adults and peers alike. She was highly motivated to work and was well liked at each of several part-time jobs.

True, Harriet suffered considerably from sharp pains in her back and joints and she frequently had severe headaches as well as recurrent ulcers on her ankles. Nevertheless, it was her social worker's opinion—an opinion that Harriet readily agreed with—that it was not her physical condition alone that accounted for her absences. Nor was it the battle for independence she waged against her mother. For weeks Harriet and her social worker conversed daily by phone. Her promises to come the next day were as easily broken as they were given. Harriet rehearsed her determination to help herself; she acknowledged the irrationality of her behavior but could not offer a convincingly satisfactory answer about why she resisted as she did. Yes, she liked the work adjustment program she was in; yes, everyone was nice to her; and yes, she would come tomorrow; but no, she honestly did not understand what was undermining her good intentions.

One day, however, during the course of their usual pleasant telephone conversation, Harriet asked, "Why is sickle cell anemia a disease of the blacks? Does this prove we are racially inferior?" Luckily, Harriet's social worker knew the facts about sickle cell anemia. She explained to Harriet the evolution of the disease from the protective function the sickle cell trait once served against malaria. Most important, she persuaded Harriet that hereditary ailments had nothing whatsoever to do with "racial inferiority," adding that the term was merely a hangover from a long since exploded myth. She went on to make clear that SCA, particularly, had its origins in geography, not in race. Harriet's voice brightened. Reassured of her worth and dignity, she stepped from the darkness of shame. A future seemed possible, if she would now avail herself of the medical options open to her.

Telephone counseling is not the usual mode. But although sickle cell anemia is common to many people, it is also an unusual disease. Whatever method persuades black people to discover whether they are victims and, if so, how they can be helped or help themselves deserves a try. Encounters with teenage patients suffering from SCA commonly reflect the scant body of knowledge and experience available about this disease. What does the patient —or, for that matter, his parent, teacher, or counselor— know about his illness? How, the adolescent wants to learn, will SCA affect his life? What are his chances of getting married, holding a job, having children? What's the use of studying history, math, or even learning to read better if he knows that he will frequently be hospitalized and suffer periods of pain? What makes one girl with mild SCA remain helpless, depressed, and unresponsive to psychological or medical help whereas another boy, perhaps suffering a more painful and debilitating sickle cell crisis, bounces back determined to claim his right to work, love, and live? Parent, teacher, and counselor must help the teenager discover affirmative answers to his negative inclination. If motivation is missing, sometimes skilled and sensitive counseling can help a youngster take a more active part in planning for his future. He can be helped to exercise his prerogative to make a choice regarding the kind of life he wishes to make for himself regardless of his disability.

Realistic explanations coupled with judicious but justifiable optimism are essential. The course of the disease is so varied that no two manifestations are identical. Occasionally, the sickling and blockage of life-giving oxygen to vital organs of the body can be so massive as to produce extensive brain damage. Happily, in most other instances, organs are far less drastically affected and it is wholly possible that many patients can live normal lives once they have been properly counseled and adequately guided toward suitable training and sensible patterns of activities. With modern medical knowledge and new treatment procedures (including chemotherapy and surgical methods) doctors and hospitals are meeting the emergency of the sickle cell crisis with far less dependency on transfusions and painkillers alone. Early attention to symptoms can do much to limit the severity and progress of the disorder as well as to ease pain and discomfort.

Aware of these possibilities, teachers, doctors, and all ancillary workers in the rehabilitation field must work together to provide the necessary hope and motivation their patients need to overcome moods of depression and hopelessness. Until new medical discoveries and genetic counseling eliminate SCA—a very real possibility—thousands of young people can be shown the way toward more productive and tolerable lives.

NOTE

1. Phenylketonuria (PKU) is an inherited metabolic disorder, which, if not corrected, can result in mental retardation.

REFERENCES

"Detecting an Old Killer," *Time* (Oct. 4, 1971): 57.

Diggs, L. W., "Sickle Cell Disease," *Journal of the American Medical Association 218* (1971): 1054.

"Discriminating Disease," *Time* (Dec. 21, 1970): 41.

Nalbandian, Robert M., "Sickle-Cell Crisis: A New Approach to Treatment," *Drug Therapy* (Feb. 1971): 56–57.

Nalbandian, Robert M., et al. "Sickledex Test for Hemoglobin S.: A Critique," *Journal of the American Medical Association 218* (1971): 1679–82.

"New Strategy for Sickle Cell Disease," *Journal of the American Medical Association 218* (1971): 1693–1694.

"Now Eddie Smith Has a Better Chance of Getting His Rhodes Scholarship," *Today's Health* (Dec. 1971): 55–56.

Scott, Robert B., "Health Care Priority and Sickle Cell Anemia," *Journal of the American Medical Association 214* (1970): 731–34.

Scott, Robert B., "Sickle-Cell Anemia—High Prevalence and Low Priority," *New England Journal of Medicine 282* (Jan. 14, 1970): 164–65.

U.S. Department of Health, Education, and Welfare, Public Health Service, "Sickle Cell Anemia—What Is It?" *Public Health Service Publication No. 1341, Health Information Series No. 119*, Washington, D.C., Government Printing Office, n.d.

Uslick, John F., D.O., "Sickle Cell Disease Associated with Beta Thalassemia: Report of a Case," *Journal of the American Osteopathic Association 69* (1970): 583–600.

4

Diabetes

The earliest clinical description of *diabetes mellitus*[1] was recorded on an Egyptian papyrus nearly 3,500 years ago. Other diagnoses of the disease appeared as the centuries passed, the stress increasingly placed upon "the sweetness of the urine,"[2] though not until the mid-eighteenth century did an English chemist discern the presence of sugar in a diabetic's urine. During the nineteenth century, researchers discovered that removing the pancreas from a dog produced diabetes. It remained for Frederick Banting and Charles Best to prove in 1921 that a de-pancreatized dog could live if it were given injections of insulin. In 1922, Banting and Best made the first successful experiment with insulin injections on a diabetic human. The era of insulin had begun.

The fifty years since that historic application are rich in dramatic contrasts with earlier history. Consider for a moment the following:

Before 1922, the diabetic suffered despair and death. Today, he may live a life of nearly normal health, his chance for happiness scarcely hindered by his physical handicap.

Before 1922, an adult diabetic's life expectancy was five to ten years. Today, many of the earliest patients treated with insulin fifty years ago are still alive. Life expectancy for diabetics is now close to that of the general population.

Before 1922, almost all children or adolescents with juvenile diabetes died within two years of the onset of the disease. Today, these young people may enjoy longer and fuller lives.

Before 1922, the only effective means of treating diabetics was a rigid starvation diet. Today, though many diabetics require diets, others are medically controlled with insulin injections or oral compounds.

Before 1922, pregnancy for a diabetic was either impossible or fatal. Today, diabetic women are normally fertile and have a better than an 85 percent chance for a safe delivery and a healthy baby.

Before 1922, diabetic patients could not be insured and were almost unemployable. Today, many insurance companies insure controlled diabetics, and industrial reports suggest that the diabetic is as good a job risk as anyone else.

Despite ample reason to rejoice, it is well to remember

also that diabetes is a serious disease, one that urgently demands prompt detection and expert care. Although diabetes is relatively easy to diagnose, routine tests for it should be requested and included in yearly checkups. Sugar in the urine, for example, though not a definitive proof of diabetes, warrants further tests for sugar in the blood.[3] Early detection can postpone or prevent dangerous complications.

Figures vary, but it is estimated that in the United States about four million people are affected by diabetes. Although it is one of the most common among chronic, noncontagious ailments, only half of these people are diagnosed as diabetics. The other half do not know they have it. About 30 percent of diabetic patients are children or adolescents with juvenile diabetes. The remaining 70 percent develop adult, or maturity-onset, diabetes. There are more than 100,000 new cases every year, and 5,600,000 persons are potentially diabetic. On the day that insulin treatment was discovered, all of these people were virtually given the gift of life.

It is important to note, too, that science does not yet know why people get diabetes. Though the precise cause or causes lie hidden, it is known that diabetes is a metabolic disorder—a consequence of too little insulin or a deficiency in insulin activity. Normally, the pancreas supplies enough of the hormone called insulin to metabolize or transform carbohydrates (sugar and starches) into energy. If these foods cannot be converted into glucose or used and stored in the usual manner, sugar accumulates in the blood and spills over into the urine. All of this, science knows. But these are processes and effects, not causes. The search for the cause is persistent and ongoing. Until that search ends triumphantly, there can be no cure for diabetes. But although no cure exists, diabetes can be controlled.

That diabetes is controllable is especially fortunate since it strikes without particular regard to nationality, race, sex, or age. However, certain individuals are, research suggests, more predisposed than others. Some reports claim a higher incidence of diabetes among Jews (two or three times more than general population) and Hindus, but attribute this to heredity rather than glandular irregularity. Doctors generally agree, too, that a tendency toward diabetes—not the disease itself—may be inherited if other members of the family have or have had the sickness. Diabetes is not, however, inherited from only one side of the family. Unless both parents are diabetic, their children are not likely to have it. If, however, a diabetic person marries a carrier of the disease (a person with the tendency toward diabetes) there is a 50 percent chance that half of their children may have diabetes. Or, if two carriers marry, one out of four children may become diabetic. Research among men and women shows that obese, middle-aged, or older women are more prone to diabetes—though exceptions in all categories, of course, do occur.

Children usually have a difficult time because their diabetes is more severe and difficult to control; they suffer more common instances of insulin reaction (too little sugar) and diabetic coma (too much sugar), and they require more care. Unhappily, despite occasional claims of "near-miracle-cures," in almost all cases where diabetes has been diagnosed during childhood, the serious, life-threatening diabetic condition and the need for insulin persists permanently. Diabetes is not a static condition. Indeed, it may change for better or for worse and therefore needs constant medical reevaluation. Clearly, then, if today's promises for better controlled diabetes are to be realized, parents of diabetic children must take full advantage of modern medical knowledge and treatment.

The six most common symptoms of diabetes are the three "polys"—polyuria, polydipsia, and polyphagia, which refer to abnormal increases in urine, thirst, and hunger—plus loss of weight, excessive fatigue, and itching. There are other symptoms, however, which are frequently and unfortunately not recognized. A person may simply not feel well and complain of general weakness. Or there may be disturbing changes in vision, delayed healing of cuts and bruises, together with persistent boils and infections. Frequently, intense itching in the genital area occurs, pain in the fingers or toes may be present, or pyorrhea and tooth decay may develop. Not all symptoms are always present; in fact, in mild cases of diabetes, there may be no symptoms at all. (No doubt this accounts for the fact that only one out of four cases of diabetes is identified and subsequently treated, while the other three cases remain unattended.) It is imperative that parents, teachers, and pediatricians be alert to the by now classical symptoms of the early stages in the development of diabetes in order to avoid potential future damage. Usually, frequent urination occurs during the day and night, together with what appears to be an insatiable thirst. Far too often, parents attribute the increased demands for soda as something "all kids want," and they are likely to assume that too much soda pop is the only reason for bed-wetting. "After all, what can you expect?" one mother complained. "He's never without soda or a drink in his hand. It's only natural that he should have to urinate more, isn't it?" If, however, the child also overeats in response to extreme hunger but loses weight, immediate medical attention is recommended.

Unfortunately, diabetes does not just go away if it is not diagnosed and treated. In fact, if a case of mild diabetes is neglected for a long period of time, definite damage occurs, such as kidney or urinary malfunctioning, even stillbirth. Excessive weight, infections, or emotional stress may also serve to activate latent diabetes. It is not known why, but uncontrolled diabetic patients, after about twenty years or so, are especially susceptible to degenerative diseases of the blood vessels. The result, in the more extreme instances, may be gangrene, heart trouble, or blindness. Today, most diabetic persons do not die of diabetes. The more rigorously a diabetic follows his doctor's instructions, the more likely he is to forestall or prevent complications. To repeat, early detection and prompt treatment of diabetes are crucial. "Complications and premature deaths are attributable almost wholly to ignorance or disregard of treatment" (Allen 1967: 54).

By far the two most serious hazards of diabetes—to which adolescents are especially vulnerable—are insulin reaction, or shock, and diabetic coma. Each of these complications can affect only those patients who are taking insulin; each has a different cause; each has different symptoms and requires different but immediate attention; and each can cause considerable damage.

Insulin reaction develops suddenly when the patient's sugar level drops too low. This may happen because he has had too much insulin, he has not eaten adequately, or he has overexerted himself physically.

Diabetic coma occurs when there is too little insulin in the body and ketosis has developed. Ketosis is a condition that results when the body uses fats for energy instead of carbohydrates. The fatty acids accumulate, poison the system, and lead to coma.

It is wise to distinguish precisely between insulin reaction and diabetic coma in order to be certain that correct treatment follows. The major differences are listed here:

INSULIN REACTION	DIABETIC COMA
Onset is sudden.	Onset is gradual.
Skin is pale and moist.	Skin is dry and hot.
Breathing is rapid and shallow.	Breathing is deep and labored.
Hunger is present; thirst is absent.	Hunger is absent; thirst is present.
Moist tongue with no breath odor.	Dry tongue and a fruity odor.
Normal frequency of urination.	Excessive urination.
Little or no sugar in the urine.	Large amounts of sugar and acetone in urine.
Strange and excited behavior.	Behavior is lethargic, patient is drowsy.

WHAT TO DO

Eat sugar, candy, crackers, soft drinks, or orange juice immediately. If symptoms do not disappear, repeat in ten minutes. If symptoms persist, call a doctor, who may inject glucose.[4]	At first signs of symptoms, notify the doctor. Rest Test urine for sugar and acetone. Inject quick-acting regular insulin. In case of severe acidosis, vomiting, extreme nausea, hospitalization may be required.

Thus far, as we have reported the facts of diabetes, we have vacillated between gloom and joy. At worst, in pre-insulin days, diabetes was a dreadful, deadly disease. At best, "present-day treatment has reduced the formerly fatal disease to a mere inconvenience" (Allen 1967: 54). What was once a major handicap for all, a tragedy for the young, is now considered by some to be an advantage. As one parent put it, "My child matured and became more independent all around once he took full responsibility for managing his diabetes." As soon as a diabetic adolescent learns to adjust to the inconveniences of diabetes, he, his parents, and his counselors can get on with the business of planning and preparing for a full vocational and social life. Rehabilitation for the diabetic patient should include plans for education, vocational training, work, marriage, and parenthood. Following are some of the facts and inconveniences the diabetic must accept.

A single, indisputable, life-or-death absolute heads the list: the need to follow treatment prescribed by a reputable doctor. In all probability (although treatment is a highly individualized matter) care for the child and youth will include at least one insulin injection daily, urine tests before breakfast and supper, a regular eating schedule, restriction of sweets, monitored physical activity, and concern for the emotional health of the patient. Specialists repeatedly warn against the dangers of letting diabetes remain uncontrolled. Some argue that a patient ages five years for every single uncontrolled year. Many believe that such complications as *diabetes neuritis* and hardening of the arteries at an early age are a direct consequence of inadequate control of diabetes. While it is true that once a diabetic, always a diabetic, it is equally true that a well-controlled diabetic gets better, whereas a poorly controlled patient tends to get worse. It is relevant also to note that insurance policies and employment are available only to controlled diabetics.

Secondly, it is important that the child and his parents understand the reasons for treatment and know everything there is to know about diabetes. There is no room for argument, appeasement, or bribery when it comes to injections, diet, tests, and the like. Naturally, caution must be exercised not to be overprotective and indulgent, overrestrictive and punitive. Every diabetic patient needs to know which precautions he must take in order to avoid additional problems. For instance, special care must be given to feet and teeth. The skin of the diabetic person is especially vulnerable to injury. Cuts, blisters, corns, calluses, athlete's foot—each, though minor, may readily develop into serious infection. The teeth of diabetic individuals also require more than the usual dental care, not because of any structural deviations, but to make certain that no abcesses or inflammations develop. Preventive measures are necessary in order to avoid infections which not only spread too rapidly and take an inordinate amount of time to heal, but also because they upset carefully balanced diabetic conditions.

And finally, the emotional climate of the family and especially the relationships between mother and child are paramount in helping the child adjust to his illness and adhere to the doctor's prescribed treatment. Parents need to know that their attitude toward diabetes and its restrictions influences the child's attitude and behavior. Obviously, the emotional health of the family is reflected in the emotional health of the child, which in turn has a profound effect upon the regulation of his disease. The family that succeeds in helping a diabetic youngster assume by the age of twelve or thirteen full responsibility for the management of his illness, and succeeds without stirring in him excessive rancor, undue rejection, or rebellion, has contributed immeasurably to his emotional and medical stability as well.

When the adolescent diabetic comes for treatment, the doctor must first bear in mind and communicate to the parents various characteristics of all adolescents. Adolescence is normally a period of sudden and rapid growth, together with increased expenditures of energy. Adolescence is also a time for increased glandular activity. Diabetic girls, for instance, frequently have additional problems associated with endocrine changes and menstrual periods. Most of us are also familiar with the delicately balanced sensibilities and frequently unbridled emotional outbursts of the adolescent. Nor are we likely to forget the urgency most teenagers feel during this period

—to become more independent, to assert themselves as individuals with the right to make their own decisions, and to live their own lives.

Other distinguishing characteristics of juvenile diabetes (the adolescent form of diabetes) are: it is more easily recognized; it is more severe; it almost always involves a deficit of insulin; it fails to discriminate between boys and girls; it disregards obesity as a predisposing factor; it is highly unstable so far as maintenance of dosage requirements and activity balance; it requires insulin injections in almost all instances; and it exhibits extreme sensitivity to insulin itself, manifested by sharp ups and downs in the level of the blood sugar.

Aware of the normal turbulences characteristic of the age group, parents should not be unduly dismayed to learn that juvenile diabetes has an acute onset and runs a stormy course. Naturally, adolescence affects diabetes, and in its turn, diabetes has a profound influence upon the adolescent. Caring for the young diabetic child creates its own special problems of maintaining regularity in all the critical areas of daily living—none of them soluble without the conscious awareness and cooperation of the patient. But the crises and complexities of the adolescent diabetic can be even more formidable. Even though a parent, and the patient too for that matter, anticipates fluctuations in the supply and demand of physical and emotional needs, it is very difficult not to become alarmed in the face of such drastic and dramatic changes. Treatment and control offer such tremendous rewards, however, that the struggle is worth every moment of arduous effort.

When diabetes is under control, the physical indicators are marked: a general feeling of well-being; maintenance of normal weight on a well-balanced diet; consistent normal blood sugars, and a maintenance of as close to normal urine sugars as is possible without acetone during the days. Five indispensable elements of treatment are necessary to attain this level of control: diet, insulin, oral compounds, exercise, and emotional attitude. The amount and kinds of insulin or oral drugs prescribed, the amount and types of food allowed, and the daily monitoring of physical activity are all interrelated and must be carefully balanced with one another in order to assure optimal effective control. Furthermore, emotional instability not only diminishes the patient's reliability to care for himself, but can result in insulin imbalance. Perhaps the most critical element in treatment, therefore, is the patient himself—and we cannot stress too emphatically the major role he plays in assuming responsibility for his welfare.

Let us begin with diet, which, along with insulin, is essential to gain optimal control of juvenile diabetes. Earlier diets, rigid and unbearably harsh and depriving, frequently approached fanatic proportions. Stories are reliably told of patients being forced to drink their own urine in order to regain lost sugar, or of an emaciated youngster who ate his toothpaste and his canary's birdseed. (Dolger and Seeman 1965: 44). For more than a decade after the use of insulin made it unnecessary to continue with such outmoded, subnormal diets, many doctors and patients nevertheless clung stubbornly to the old diet cults.

Pediatricians were the first to rebel against forcing dangerously undernourishing diets upon children. Even though these children received insulin and had their sugar metabolism restored to normal functioning, they remained underweight and underdeveloped, lagging far behind the normal growth patterns of healthy children their age. Physicians prescribed a more standard diet for diabetic children, urging that they had the same nutritional needs as any other child—except for the restriction of sugars. They argued that all children, whether diabetic or not, must have proper proportions of protein, carbohydrates, and fats, and they must have enough vitamins and minerals in their foods if they are to grow properly.

Obviously, more calories are needed (about twice as many as when one is fully grown) to keep pace with the spurts of physical growth, increased activities, and glandular changes of the adolescent years. Diabetic instability may be characteristic of juvenile diabetes, but a cooperative patient and a persistent doctor can arrive at an appetizing menu which includes snacks and follows a consistent pattern from day to day. Modern diabetic diets stress regularity with a restriction of those foods which have heavy concentrations of sugar (candy, soda, jelly, and jam). Some ice cream, puddings, and cookies are allowed on occasion (carbohydrates should be limited to 200 grams a day), provided overweight does not become a problem.

Contrary to popular belief, diabetic meals do not have to become monotonous. With the aid of exchange lists (instead of the tedious old practice of scales and measurements) there is no end to the variety of foods permissible. Here, for example, is a recommendation from the American Diabetic Association:

Here's how the exchanges work. If the diet calls for one slice of bread with a meal, the lists show that instead of the bread the diabetic may choose one of a good many other items—among them half a cup of cooked cereal, half a cup of rice or macaroni, half a cup of lima beans or split peas, half an ear of corn, or a small baked potato. Or he may drop the bread and have vanilla ice cream for dessert—an eighth of a quart—if he also omits two fat exchanges, which are equivalent of two level teaspoons of butter.

Among the items the diabetic may use freely are coffee and tea (without sugar or cream), clear broth, fat-free bouillon, and unsweetened gelatin, cranberries, and pickle. Without overstepping his diet he may also use ordinary amounts of a good many vegetables. Some of these are asparagus, cabbage, cauliflower, cucumber, eggplant, beet greens, kale, lettuce, rhubarb, sauerkraut, young string beans, summer squash, and tomatoes [*Facts About Diabetes* 1966].

To summarize, the object of diet in the treatment of today's diabetic adolescent is to provide a consistent eating schedule, limit carbohydrates, allow for sufficient daily nutrition, and prevent future obesity.

The second critical aspect of treatment is insulin injections—practically a "must" for all adolescent juvenile diabetics. For them, as for hundreds of thousands afflicted with diabetes, insulin has revoked an otherwise certain death sentence. Insulin is not a cure and it is not the final word in treatment, but it is the most satisfactory source of treatment and control now available. A natural hormone, insulin can be administered only by injection. Otherwise, as when taken orally, the digestive juices of the stomach destroy its efficacy. An extremely potent but nonaddictive substance, a single teaspoonful of pure insulin can medicate a severe diabetic for more than five years. The quality and uniform strength of insulin are tested and certified by the Food and Drug Administration of the United States; the quantity needed should be determined only by a doctor and depends upon the severity of the diabetes, the nature of the patient's diet, and his pattern of activity.

Since the days of its original discovery, when four injections a day were not uncommon in severe cases of diabetes, new kinds of insulin have been developed. Basically, there are three types of insulin: plain or fast-acting insulins, which reduce the amount of sugar within two to four hours but lose their effect rapidly; intermediate insulins, which take from eight to twelve hours to attain their full potency but retain some effect for twenty-four hours; and slow-acting insulins, which take from eighteen to twenty-four hours before they become maximally effective but maintain some effects for another twenty-four hours. Such a variety of insulins have made it possible to accommodate the varying needs of patients —from a single injection of one type of insulin a day to any number of combinations of several types of insulins.

The diabetic should have on hand at all times adequate supplies of the proper equipment:

1. The correct type of insulin (plus an extra vial) kept under refrigeration for emergencies.

2. The correct syringe for the U40 or U80 insulin (plus an extra one in case of loss or breakage).

3. A sharp hypodermic needle and a reserve supply.

4. A sterile case for storage and travel.

5. Ordinary alcohol and sterile cotton for use at the time of injection.

6. A supply of sugar or glucagon preparation in case of an insulin reaction.

7. A supply of daily tests for sugar (Clinitest, Clinistix, Tes-Tape or Uristix), as well as a supply of daily tests for urinary acetone (Ketostix, Acetest).

8. Every diabetic should always have on his person his name, address, phone number, and a clear identification of his illness together with instructions in case of insulin shock or coma:

> If I am unconscious or behaving abnormally I may be having an insulin reaction. If I can swallow, give me sugar, candy, fruit juice or a sweetened drink. If I cannot swallow or do not recover promptly, call a physician and send me to the hospital at once [Dolger and Seeman 1965: 86].

Let us pause briefly to consider the most recent treatment used in certain cases of diabetes: the oral compounds (Orinase and Diabinese are the most widely known). Insulin, although indispensable, creates diverse problems. The very young, the very old, and the infirm may not be able to accomplish self-injection; the hazards of insulin shock and coma are omnipresent; occasional resistance or allergy to insulin may develop; and rigid mealtime schedules are for many an irritant and a nuisance. Efforts to discover a safe, effective, and inexpensive substitute began coincident with the discovery of insulin.[5] Since 1955, the oral substitutes, as they are sometimes called, have been in use.

The new oral drugs, however, are not true substitutes for insulin. They can be used only by a patient capable of producing some insulin within his own system, and the oral drugs work very differently from insulin. The precise manner in which the oral compounds function has not yet been determined, but they do reduce high counts of blood sugar, assist in metabolizing sugars and starches, and are generally considered to be, within limits, safe and effective (U.S. Department of H., E., and W. 1966: 113). What is already certain, however, is that not all types of diabetes may be treated with oral compounds. Almost without exception, their use is restricted to adults. The oral compounds are not, at this time, considered to be suitable for the treatment of adolescent diabetics. Furthermore, they do not work in the treatment of diabetic coma, when surgery is needed, or when a serious infection is present.

Researchers hope within the foreseeable future to develop oral drugs for the young. Meanwhile, the oral drugs are helping others by eliminating the danger of insulin shock and keeping urine free of sugar. From the patient's point of view, the new drug is easier and more convenient to administer. Some physicians add that when oral compounds work, they work even better than insulin for some patients. A not inconsiderable byproduct of research on oral drugs is that investigators may learn more about how insulin works, what the causes of diabetes are, and how it may be cured and/or prevented.

Physical activity is another component always mentioned in connection with treatment of the diabetic and is as frequently misunderstood as diet. More harm than good may come from starvation diets as well as from arbitrary limitation of all physical activity. This does not, however, mean that exercise does not need to be regulated and balanced with other facets of treatment. Sugar and starch turn into glucose and/or energy in the body. Exercise helps the body use up some of this excess energy. Aware of the physiological process, the diabetic must recognize the need to act and exercise. For a diabetic teenager, it is urgent that he know he risks insulin shock if he does not take the necessary precautions of eating candy or drinking soda before engaging in any athletic event, gym period, and the like. Parents should encourage their teenage son or daughter to participate fully in gym and other sports, in fact in all the usual physical and social activities that interest their friends. They can run, bicycle, jump, swim, skate, and have even more exhausting exercise so long as they remember to consume extra sweets and know all the facts that contribute to their maintaining a particular stability level. They must be educated to know how much exercise is too much or too little, how much extra food is necessary to prevent an insulin reaction, and the like. Not to know is to court insulin shock or diabetic coma. Dr. William Kennedy recommends a consistent daily pattern of activity. Indeed he warns that consistency is the order of the day in every phase of treatment: insulin, food, mealtimes, and emotional response.

There is nothing abnormal about the youngster whose energy is expended in a changeable pattern. The patient and those who deal with him must learn to recognize and anticipate the effects of various degrees and kinds of activity, so that stability may be maintained by appropriate measures. For example, one patient determined by rough trial and error that an average set of tennis required 15 gm. of extra carbohydrate, plus or minus 5 to 10 gm. for strenuous or mild sets. He could maintain control sitting at a desk in school during the week, and continue adequate balance during a full Saturday afternoon of tennis by consuming orange juice or sugar lumps in appropriate amounts between sets. To deny the young diabetic any desired form of reasonably normal activity is to create a harmful situation. Cautious experiment and learning through experience provide the means for control and avoid the hazards [Kennedy 1955: 207].

That Dr. Kennedy's advice has worked is notably evident in the highly energetic and successful careers of Billy Talbert and Ham Richardson, two famous tennis players who have had diabetes since childhood.

Not until insulin treatment helped diminish concern for a diabetic's survival did specialists begin seriously to attend to psychological and emotional problems related to the disease. Diabetes mellitus is, as one authority writes, "One of the organic disorders in which the importance of emotional factors had been recognized for a long time, although this knowledge was overshadowed for a while by one-sided interest in physiologic aspects" (Bruch 1949: 200–210).

Although no evidence exists for a distinctive diabetic personality profile, there is little doubt that the personality of the diabetic person is significantly affected by the disease. Personality reactions and adjustments to diabetic regulations vary widely, ranging from a compulsive, orderly, inflexible person to a timid, apprehensive, anxious, vulnerable individual; from a rebellious, aggressive, self-destructive delinquent to someone who is depressed, dependent, and passive. Combinations of these and other traits are equally possible. The sources of psychic distress in the diabetic adolescent are not difficult to locate. One simply does not adapt easily to the reality of living with diabetes or just get used to it. Having diabetes is, as Newman writes, like being in a state of "constant awareness of danger" (Newman 1963: 425–33). One of the most obvious points of trauma is the daily regimen of injection, a wellspring of both fear and shame. The injection itself stirs dread, as does the specter of insulin reaction or coma. Then, too, there is the shame many youngsters feel about injecting themselves at school or at a friend's home. Often, injections are thus delayed, or, worse, skipped altogether.

Rigid controls—injection, dietary restriction, urine tests—are another provocative cause of emotional disturbances. Frequently adolescents use their illness to rebel against parental authority—at the risk of their own lives. It is a time for parental patience, understanding, and tolerance, not simply for unbending discipline. Food is a typical signal for emotional upset. Teenagers are always hungry, but the diabetic youth has a special problem. He knows that insulin stability depends on regulated meals, but he does not wish to be thought "different" by his friends at the local ice-cream stand. Nor does he want to feel guilty about betraying his promise to his parents to stick to his diet. Inevitably, he will on occasion break the rules. More important is that he not develop neurotic attitudes toward eating itself. As a report from the U.S. Health Department advises, food should not serve as a "solace, as a substitute for love, or as a release from anxiety" (U.S. Department of H., E., and W. 1966: 13).

Other adolescents find the daily urine tests objectionable. Some diabetic girls develop strong feelings against taking urine tests during their menstrual periods. "Really, mother," one girl protested, "it's just too much!"

Complaints and refusals notwithstanding, injections, urine tests, and dietary controls must prevail. Once the adolescent concedes these skirmishes, he has a fine chance to win the war itself. The triumph is psychic as well as physical, for to achieve a satisfactory adjustment to diabetes is to demonstrate "discipline, will power, self-control, integrity, and an optimistic attitude—qualities which, in themselves, help to build good character. Well-controlled diabetics display such qualities as health, intelligence, self-reliance, and happiness to a degree above that exhibited by their colleagues whose metabolic processes are normal" (Kennedy 1955: 209).

Personality studies of diabetic adolescents and of family attitude toward the illness indicate how wide-ranging both traits and relationships may be—and how intimately they are intertwined. In an emotionally stable family environment, Bruch reports (1949: 204), there is evidence of the child's healthy acceptance of his illness as well as cooperation and understanding. Where shame, guilt, and hostility prevail, there are also rebellion, recalcitrance, and dependency. One mother adhered rigidly to the medical regimen, boasting that her daughter was "very well trained." The price—submission and passivity. Another mother shared her son's refusal to acknowledge the seriousness of his affliction. She coddled his carelessness about diet, changed doctors and schools. Physically, he deteriorated; psychically and academically, he fell into deep trouble.

Karen

The case of Karen is worth detailing. A seventeen-and-a-half-year-old, Karen was first diagnosed as being diabetic at the age of ten. During a recent conference, Karen matter of factly recited her troubles of the past five years —recurrent conjunctivitis, frequent episodes of sinus infections, hospitalizations for peptic ulcer, diabetic coma, and an appendectomy operation just three months ago. Given such a preponderance of complications, Karen seemed almost too well adjusted. Yes, she understood that her eye trouble was probably related to the diabetes and that sinus infections could cause insulin imbalance.

"What a lousy break," she added, "getting an ulcer on top of diabetes and having *two* diets to follow—ugh! I found out the hard way that you can have diabetes *plus* an ulcer, *plus* an operation. . . . At least in these respects I'm just like anyone else."

Here was a young lady well versed in the dynamics of how to be a model diabetic patient. But did she know how serious her condition truly was? She administered her own insulin injections and faithfully followed her physician's instructions regarding diet, daily urine tests, and exercise.

"Otherwise, I have no problems," she insisted. "I can do anything anyone else can do."

To her counselor, however, it seemed that Karen did far less than others. At home, she avoided daily chores with familiar complaints. "My sugar is too high . . . my stomach aches . . . I feel dizzy. Perhaps I had better lie down for a while." Frequent absences and broken appointments with her rehabilitation counselor seemed to raise doubts about her constant assurances that "Everything is okay. I'm fine and under good control." Was Karen's diabetes really stabilized? Or was she, perhaps, malingering? When the counselor wisely discussed the situation with the doctor, he learned that Karen was indeed an ideal patient.

"Furthermore," the doctor assured her counselor, "her diabetes *is* reasonably well controlled, considering the usual ups and downs of the adolescent juvenile diabetic. Malingering? Not a chance. Not Karen. She had quite a scare, you know. We almost lost her this past summer when she had surgery for her appendix. Give her time, she'll work it out and come back fighting. She's entitled to a period of being overly careful after what she's gone through."

Before the operation, Karen had doggedly worked every day at her first job as a salesgirl, despite persistent stomach pains. Differential diagnosis between acidosis and an emergency condition which requires surgery is sometimes difficult enough to make. But Karen's stoicism and determination "not to give in" actually delayed the operation and substantially increased the risk of a successful outcome. Luckily, Karen kept a routine checkup appointment and her doctor's prompt action probably saved her life.[6]

Assured that Karen was realistic about the seriousness of her condition and responsible toward her own care, the counselor could proceed with deeper understanding and increased optimism. Karen's good sense prevailed. Through the years, she followed her regimen faithfully until it became almost second nature. She was a good example of the diabetic patient who turns her disability into an advantage. Her courage and confidence served her well at work and prepared her to meet the challenge of marriage and motherhood.

Yes, motherhood, though had Karen lived in pre-insulin days, she would not have had the chance to be a mother—for at that time, most diabetic women were sterile. Even after the discovery of insulin, diabetic women who conceived and managed to have a normal pregnancy either delivered stillborn babies or the infant died shortly after birth. Doctors today, however, claim that the chances of a diabetic woman having a healthy baby are far greater than they were forty years ago—if her doctor approves, if her husband is not diabetic, and if she is willing and able to cooperate fully. Today, a diabetic woman need not hesitate to become pregnant so long as she is intimately familiar with the diabetic way of life and understands how her diabetes will influence the course of pregnancy. Pregnancy may temporarily alter diabetic stability but, in the long run, will not affect the severity of the disease. Expert diabetic and obstetrical attention are required from the start, beginning with pre-pregnancy tests (lung, X-ray, blood counts, and examination of the heart and kidney). Modifications in diet and insulin therapy should also be anticipated. For those women who developed diabetes when they were very young or have had it for a long time, female hormones will probably be prescribed in order to minimize the chance of miscarriage or kidney poisoning, and to enhance the likelihood of the baby's surviving after delivery. Some physicians encourage early delivery whenever the slightest obstetrical deviance exists and pay special attention also to the breathing and blood sugar of newborn infants of diabetic mothers. Occasionally, an incubator is recommended in order to make the first few days as easy as possible for the infant.

Diabetic mothers can be encouraged to have children (though no more than two, usually) provided they are thoroughly aware of the seriousness of the situation and are ready to accept the responsibilities attendant upon their decision.

Brian

Brian, a nineteen-year-old, pale, slight youth endured a set of related diabetic complaints totally different from Karen's. Perhaps because his diabetic condition was mild, he erroneously concluded that he need not follow the doctor's instructions too carefully. Although he continued with his insulin, he neglected his diet and urine tests. Consequently, Brian frequently experienced periods of uncontrolled diabetes that invariably led to bouts of diabetic neuritis. The first time, Brian was hospitalized for a month until his diabetes could be brought under satisfactory control and the related symptoms and pain of neuritis alleviated. During that time he lost his appetite and a great deal of weight and also fell far behind in his schoolwork. Thereafter, whenever Brian suffered from pain in his arms and legs, or had feelings of numbness in his fingers or toes—early symptoms which he had previously neglected—he hastily put himself on a rigid diet, faithfully tested his urine, and was relieved to note that within a few days his blood sugar dropped to a normal level and, thereafter, that he was free from pain.

Brian realized that extended periods of uncontrolled diabetes almost always cause diabetic neuritis. Predictably, however, Brian reverted to his careless eating habits. Because he did not recognize other signs of *diabetes neuritis*—diarrhea, constipation, or certain muscular weaknesses, i.e. in the eyes or the toes—he did not always take immediate action to correct his diabetic imbalance. As a result, his condition persisted, pain and discomfort lingered, and relief was delayed for months. Once, when visited in the hospital, Brian solemnly promised, "I've learned my lesson. Never again. From now on I stick to my diet. Just watch and see if I don't." Sadly, the record reports otherwise: recurrent periods of uncontrolled diabetes followed by prolonged treatment for diabetic neuritis. Inevitably, Brian will pay the price for uncontrolled diabetes with permanent damage to his legs or feet and, possibly, the onset of early vascular problems.

Emily

One last case history calls attention to the problem of the diabetic and his place in the job market. Times have changed markedly since the pre-insulin era when the diabetic had so many restrictions upon his activities that employment was ever a remote possibility. Even today, employers are apprehensive—and rightly so—about the possibility of insulin shock. But industry has gradually grown less resistant to hiring a person with diabetes (especially during World War II, when there was a shortage of workers) provided that his condition is controlled and that he agrees to regular medical examinations.[7]

Pert and petite seventeen-year-old Emily was astonished at the suggestion that she look for part-time employment. "Who would hire me? I'm diabetic." Emily had responded with the same incredulity when her willingness, cooperativeness, and diligence in learning typing, shorthand, and filing won praise from her vocational evaluator. Her dependability and capability were as steady and unwavering as her strong belief that she was worthless, would never be taken seriously by an employer, boy friend or, for that matter, her family either. On the surface, Emily's problem of self-doubt appeared to be simple, but in practice many months were to pass before her self-image matched her competency.

For years she had unquestioningly accepted her role as the "sick one" in the family. Underdeveloped physically, slow in school because of frequent absences, considered a nuisance because of her special food and insulin requirements, Emily was even referred to by her brothers and sisters as retarded. No one had ever bothered to notice the wide discrepancy between the little that was expected of Emily and the formidable services that she actually performed daily. Since the death of her mother three years earlier, quietly and without complaint, Emily had cared for her younger sisters and had taken over household chores generally, cleaning, shopping, and cooking. Yet her father's conviction that Emily could never have a normal life of work and marriage became her own. So ingrained was the family's misguided faith in her limitations that it took considerable time and deft persuasion before Emily's father permitted her (and Emily agreed) to register and participate in a vocationally oriented personal adjustment rehabilitation program. Gradually, Emily's appearance, clothes, and outlook reflected her improved self-esteem. Despite the general attitude that juvenile diabetics are considered poor employment risks, Emily's skills, her performance on her first job, together with an excellent attendance record and no accidents, soon led to full-time employment as a secretary.

Naturally, not all diabetics find employment this readily. Complications frequently arise which make placement more difficult. When a company policy is to hire controlled diabetics, for example, the firm usually recommends that those who must eat regularly or take insulin on schedule had best avoid positions which have rotating shifts. Personnel officials know too that diabetics are susceptible to infections and avoid assigning them jobs which involve high risk of physical injury. Vocational planners should also bear in mind the need to avoid situations likely to create emotional tension. Certain positions are never recommended, for obvious reasons—airplane pilot or truck driver, for example. But within these guidelines a diabetic should be encouraged to apply for whatever job he is qualified to perform satisfactorily.

NOTES

1. *Diabetes insipidus,* a disease caused by the malfunctioning of the pituitary gland, is not related to *diabetes mellitus.*

2. *Diabetes* is of Greek origin, meaning "to pass through." *Mellitus* is of Latin origin, meaning "honey." Thus, the frequent references to "the sweetness of the urine."

3. The sugar content of the blood, when diabetes is present, may range from a low of 60 mg percent after fasting, to a high of 160 mg after eating—as compared with a range of 100 to 105 mg percent for normal blood sugar level. In the event that no sugar is present in the blood, but a high level of sugar persists in the urine, other nondiabetic disturbances may be indicated, i.e. toxic goiter, tumor of the adrenal or pituitary glands, brain injury, or renal diabetes. The latter is a benign kidney disorder which requires no treatment or diet and does not develop into *diabetes mellitus.*

4. In 1960 glucagon became the second protein hormone to be chemically characterized—insulin was the first. It brought prompt relief to insulin reactions.

5. The extraordinary feat of synthesizing insulin chemically was first accomplished in 1966 by Dr. P. Katsogannis and others. This was the first human hormone and the most intricate protein ever to be manufactured artificially. However, it is not yet available for treatment as an oral insulin.

6. Today's diabetics can undergo operations and tolerate any type of anesthesia. Moreover, they share the same protection as other nondiabetic patients from infections, because of antibiotics such as penicillin and other drugs.

7. Before 1941, the federal government would not hire diabetics, but the 1956 U.S. Civil Service Commission states: "That persons with controlled diabetes may be good employees and that it is good business to hire them. . . . a diabetic is capable of safe and efficient services in an appropriate job, provided satisfactory control of his condition is maintained . . . [mild] diabetics are capable of performing any type of work for which they are otherwise qualified . . . more severe diabetics . . . should not require work in heights or around dangerous power driven machinery, work involving the operation of motor vehicles . . ." (U.S. Civil Service Commission 1956).

REFERENCES

Allen, Frederick M., "Diabetes Mellitus," in *Encyclopedia Americana 9*, New York, Americana Corp. (1967): 54.

Bruch, Hilde, "Physiologic and Psychologic Interrelationships in Diabetes in Children," *Psychosomatic Medicine 11* (1949): 200–210.

Dolger, Henry, and Bernard Seeman, *How to Live with Diabetes*, New York, W. W. Norton, 1965.

Facts About Diabetes, New York, American Diabetes Association, 1966.

Kennedy, W. B., "Psychologic Problems of the Young Diabetic," *Diabetes 4* (1955): 207–209.

Newman, Joseph, "Psychological Problems of Children and Youth with Chronic Medical Disorders," in *Psychology of Exceptional Children and Youth*, 2d ed., William M. Cruickshank, ed., Englewood Cliffs, N.J., Prentice-Hall, 1963: 394–447.

U.S. Civil Service Commission, *Employment of Diabetics in the Federal Service*, Washington, D.C., Government Printing Office, 1956.

U.S. Department of Health, Education, and Welfare, Social and Rehabilitation Service, Rehabilitation Services Administration, *A Survey of Medicine and Medical Practice for the Rehabilitation Counselor*, Washington, D.C., Government Printing Office, 1966.

5

Allergies
and Asthma

Allergy is an atypical or hypersensitive reaction to certain substances called allergens or antigens (these terms are broad and interchangeable, referring simply to substances that cause allergy). More than 18 million Americans suffer, according to estimates, from one or another of the allergic ailments that involve the respiratory or nervous systems, gastrointestinal tract, skin, eyes and ears, heart and blood vessels, blood, or connective tissues —in fact, any organ of the body. In this chapter, we shall examine three of those allergies that are particularly likely to engage the attention of the teacher, parent, or the rehabilitation counselor: skin allergies, hay fever, and asthma.

Some allergies are mild and cause little strain; others are severe and are responsible for physical pain and psychic tension. None of the allergies are contagious, but they are often inherited, though one need not inherit sensitivity to the same allergen that brought discomfort to his parent. Except for the quirks of inheritance, however, many doctors believe (though still without definitive evidence) that people who develop allergies are constitutionally different from those who do not. Perhaps the most important generalization that can be made concerns the age groupings of allergy victims—and even here it is necessary to hedge. Although allergy may appear at any age, it is statistically the fourth among chronic diseases affecting children. Furthermore, children between the ages of five and fifteen show the greatest predisposition toward allergy (and, more than a third of these go without medical care). And finally, most allergies can be traced to childhood origins.

If the disorder is diagnosed and treated properly as soon as possible after its onset, prospects for a permanent cure—that is, elimination of the cause—are greatly enhanced. Treatments such as desensitization and the use of drugs often yield complete relief, ending all symptoms and any occasion for further treatment. But because one does not outgrow allergy, many people will always require medical care. Should the allergy remain undiagnosed and untreated in childhood, the likelihood is that it will persist. Yet worse, it may spread and affect other tissues or organs (then known as shock tissue or shock organ) with serious complications that may lead to hay fever, asthma, kidney disease, or heart trouble. The allergic child can grow into a healthy, normal adult if effective treatment is administered before it is too late. Indifference during the early stages of allergy far too often results in permanent physical damage, personality difficulties, and, in exceptional cases, death.

It is impossible to itemize all of the countless agents (dust, drugs, food, bacteria, and the like) responsible for specific allergies. But many of the most common offenders are known. We inhale pollen, mold spores, house and insect dust, animal danders, and much else; we swallow foods such as eggs, milk, fish, wheat, and conventional drugs such as aspirin; we touch dyes, cosmetics, chemicals and metals; we are injected with medicines such as penicillin and insulin, and involuntarily, by the stings of wasps and bees; or we may even become sensitized to some of our own internal bacteria and tissues. Obviously, these substances are natural and harmless products for most people, and are certainly not to be avoided unless a physician proves by test the presence of an allergic response. It is perfectly normal to sneeze if the nostrils are assailed by dust when a carpet is beaten. It is equally likely and normal that digestive discomfort—which is not at all necessarily the same as an allergy—may follow after eating spicy or fried foods. Many nonallergic people suffer from indigestion. The allergic person is one who responds abnormally to what others experience as commonplace. When the truly allergic person has eaten eggs, or patted a dog, he may find himself covered with hives or gasping for breath.

Much remains to be learned about how an allergy develops and what occurs before symptoms appear. But we are not completely in the dark. We know that allergy existed as early as 2641 B.C. because the death of King Menes was recorded on Egyptian hieroglyphic tablets as caused by a hornet's "bite." Since that time, references have been found in Lucretius and in the Babylonian Talmud describing allergies and the practice of building up tolerance to certain foods that had caused distress. Hippocrates, for example, advised against giving milk to anyone with a "sick headache" (migraine) (Harris and Shure 1969: 1). In the nineteenth century two English physicians, John Bostock and Charles Blackley (hay fever and asthma sufferers), performed tests on themselves that ultimately led to the recognition and description of the connection between vegetation and allergy. In 1911 Doctors Noon and Freeman of London began treatment of pollen-induced hay fever and asthma, approximating the "desensitization treatment" used today (Harris and Shure 1969: 7).

Although many questions remain, some facts about certain allergic processes are understood. For one thing, more than a single exposure to a substance is necessary before allergy develops. Another crucial point concerns the interaction between antibodies and allergens. Laymen rightly assume that antibodies (which are always naturally available in blood serum) battle against toxicity. But in allergic reactions, the antibody is not a friendly agent. When an allergen enters the body, it stimulates the production of antibodies. Exposed for a second time to the same allergen, the antibody joins with it to effect the release of histamine (or other chemicals) from the cells and to create the allergic symptom. The particular locus of the allergic reaction depends upon where the chemical reaction—known as the antigen-antibody reaction—takes place. If it is on the skin, the allergic symptoms may be hives; if in the nose, hay fever;

and if in the involuntary muscles of the bronchial tubes, asthma.

An important function of the diagnosis of allergy is to establish the cause and adopt the proper course of treatment. The allergist or a laboratory technician customarily performs a series of allergy skin tests to help discover the cause. Interpretation of these skin tests requires a trained allergist, one with broad knowledge and experience. Although these tests are safe and painless, simple to administer, and invaluable for diagnosis, occasionally they too fail to identify a cause definitively (Feinberg 1968: 132). Most doctors, however, find the skin tests both reliable and necessary.

The *scratch test* is most commonly used—especially with the very young because it is so simple, quick, and convenient. Many "scratches" on the back (between the shoulder blades) can be accomplished at one sitting. Small amounts of selected antigens, in powdered or liquid form, are rubbed on the scratch. If the patient is sensitive or allergic to a particular substance, a small, mosquito-bite-like hive will appear after a few minutes. When scratch tests are negative, physicians may test further by introducing the antigen between the layers of the skin on the outside of the upper arm with very fine needles. This intradermal procedure is slightly more difficult to perform, but it is not painful and it is more sensitively responsive to the allergen. Sometimes, when a patient cannot come to the office for tests, or if his skin is too sensitive or is already otherwise affected by a skin disease, the allergist may use *passive-transfer* tests. Here, very reliable results are obtained by injecting blood taken from the allergic patient, within the layers of the skin of a nonallergic person. Although there is no danger of transferring the allergy and the process is thoroughly safe, the passive-transfer test is used less frequently than others because of the inconveniences and difficulties involved. *Patch tests* are commonly used when contact with a suspected substance is believed to be the allergic cause. For instance, a sample of a particular substance may be applied to the inner surface of the forearm, covered, and left in place for about two to four days to determine whether or not the individual has an allergenic response to that substance. Other available tests are far less commonly used. The *conjunctival test, nasal instillation test, nasal inhalation* or "sniff test," *bronchial inhalation test*—all take too much time to administer, cause more severe reactions, and generally discomfit the patient.

Skin tests are rarely the sole basis for diagnosing an allergy. Interactions among allergy, infection, and emotional disturbance; symptoms, frequency, duration, and intensity of attacks; and details of the patient's personal medical history are all necessary for a reliable diagnosis (Harris and Shure 1969: 35).

SKIN ALLERGIES

Some doctors refer metaphorically to our skin as the largest of all our organs. Certainly it is vulnerable to a host of external and internal allergens that may cause allergy. The spectrum of common skin allergies is full, and each allergy requires differential diagnosis and discriminated treatment. Three of these are discussed here, each a familiar outcropping of discomfort that should

stir awareness as well as compassion in an alert counselor. Of the three—hives, contact dermatitis, and eczema—one, eczema, has sufficiently dramatic psychological effects to warrant the inclusion here of a case history.

Hives

A hive (or urticaria) is a swelling that occurs when
enlarged blood vessels leak fluids from a white raised
center (wheal) encircled by an area of redness. Chemically, hives are caused by an alteration of the blood vessels. The location of shock tissue determines whether the
manifestation will be a single hive or a broader area of
swelling—eye, lip, or, internally, painful swollen joints
or muscles. Often, other symptoms such as fever, vomiting, or cramps may also be present *(The Skin and Its
Allergies* 1966: 3).

Hives may be small or large, surface singly or in clus-
ters, last only briefly or linger for weeks, months, or
years. What causes the chemical reaction? Too often,
there is no identifiable cause. But we do know that many
result from food (nuts, fish, milk, strawberries), drugs
(penicillin, aspirin, certain laxatives and pain-killers), insect bites, and even from parasites in the gastro-intesti-
nal tract. Most hives produce an immediate reaction:
surface hives itch; inner hives, though not itchy, cause
pain in the joints, muscles, throat, and the like.

Treatment and relief of acute hives are simple and
swift once the cause has been discovered and eliminated.
Chronic cases, on the other hand, take longer to cure,
persisting until the specific cause can be tracked down.
When the condition persists, the search for the cause

becomes more difficult and involves close and continuous scrutiny of habitually taken foods, laxatives, vitamins, or medicines. Skin tests are rather less helpful than usual with stubborn cases because of their limited reliability with food or with the drugs that may cause hives. Emotional problems should be investigated by a psychiatrist if necessary, but only to be identified as a contributing, aggravating factor—*not* as the cause.

Effective relief from symptoms is possible with the use of antihistamines, soothing creams and lotions, or baths (using starch, baking soda, or bran). In severe cases, physicians may prescribe cortisone (or cortisone-like products) or an adrenaline injection—either of which usually brings quick relief. A few other methods of treatment—autohemotherapy (injection of the patient's own blood into his vessels) or inducement of high fever—may terminate chronic attacks, though how they do so remains a mystery.

Contact Dermatitis

Though it is not primarily an allergy that affects adolescents, contact dermatitis deserves brief mention not only because of the countless number of everyday objects to which hundreds of thousands of people are allergic, but also because it has such a profound and increasing effect upon industrial workers. More than 100,000 workers in the U. S. have occupational dermatitis and lose millions of workdays annually because they are allergic to the products they must handle: dyes, plastics, resins, rubber, metals, and specific chemicals. Nor is occupational dermatitis limited to such industries. Workers who handle certain drugs (cocaine, novocaine, sulfa, penicillin) are affected, as are those who handle synthetics in textile and clothing factories, or metals in jewelry making, or the oils and dyes in cosmetics.

Contact dermatitis is the generic name for all of those externally acquired allergies that depend upon actual contact between the allergen and the skin. The most familiar forms of "skin poisoning" are the "summer afflictions"—poison ivy, poison oak, and poison sumac. No one "catches" this allergy by being near a plant. There must be contact, though one's clothing or the dog he is walking may indirectly result in contact. There are many other plants—outdoor as well as indoor varieties—that have been identified as causes of contact allergy. Ragweed plants are foremost among outdoor plants which contain substances in the leaf and pollen (not the same part of the ragweed which produces hay fever allergy) that produce contact allergy. It is virtually impossible to enumerate all of the house plants, vegetables, and fruits known to have caused contact dermatitis at one time or another to certain individuals. And it is little comfort to learn that plant life is just one small source contributing to the total number of people who develop contact allergy.

Practically all cosmetics, deodorants, hair preparations, men's toilet items, and detergents—or some one ingredient of these products—are frequently isolated as having caused contact allergic reactions. Dyes used in furs, shoes, or clothing may cause skin allergies. Metals used in jewelry and silverware and even in hooks and eyes, zippers, and dentures have caused inflammations.

Rash and itching are the main symptoms, but when

contact ceases, the rash disappears and the itching stops. The treatment is deceptively simple: remove the cause. In some instances sensitization to offending substances may alleviate the situation or washing with soap and water after exposure may avoid trouble. At other times, cotton-lined rubber gloves or the application of medically prescribed ointments and lotions is effective; anti-itching drugs also may be used. In extreme cases, cortisone products may be prescribed. While it is easy to stay away from ivy, oak, and sumac, the difficulties for the industrial worker are readily apparent but not so readily avoidable. As new materials are discovered, new allergens will cause new rashes. No overall solution to this problem seems imminent or likely.

Eczema (topic dermatitis)

Eczema is the allergic form most common in infants and should be attended with utmost diligence lest it spread, cause infection, or be followed by pneumonia. In a young child eczema is recognized by the moist rash on cheeks, scalp, arms, or legs. In very bad cases, the rash may become a cluster of small blisters that break and release fluid (a condition known as "weeping"). The skin then is likely to thicken and crust over as it dries.

The young patient is usually allergic to foods, but as he becomes older, he is more vulnerable to those allergens which are airborne (pollen, dust, animal hairs, feathers) or to infectious agents (serums, antibiotics). He is also likely to display symptoms of hay fever and asthma as well. Among children, eczema may cause loss of sleep, irritability, and lowered resistance. The adoles-

cent or young adult afflicted with eczema may develop
psychological, social, or vocational problems, which in
turn may aggravate the skin condition, become a contributing cause, and set the stage for circular recurrence.
For the most part, eczema does not persist after childhood, though it may occasionally reappear in different
forms as the child gets older.

Opinions vary about whether or not eczema is a true
allergy. Harris and Shure (1969: 213) list six different possible causes:

1. A disturbance of the normal mechanism of perspira-
tion with collection of the sweat in the bends of the
elbows and knees.

2. A nonallergic illness that happens to occur in people who have allergies such as hay fever and asthma.

3. An allergy to oneself or to one's own skin.

4. A purely allergic disease (like hay fever).

5. An emotional disease with scratching as the cause of
the rash.

6. An inborn disease of enzyme metabolism.

Treatment usually begins with a few general injunc-
tions: avoid direct contact with wool, rough cloth, dog or
cat hairs, sudden changes in hot or cold temperature, dry
air, and excessive soap and water; remove all feather
pillows, rugs, and carpets from the bedroom; don't
scratch—it increases both the itch and the possibility of
infection. Eliminating or avoiding the allergen is, of
course, the most desirable course to pursue. Certain all-
ergy-causing foods must be omitted altogether. In some
cases of allergy, cooked or canned foods are less allergenic than raw foods. In any event, the diet must be
carefully supervised by a physician to assure adequate

intake of protein, calories, minerals, and vitamins *(The Skin and Its Allergies* 1966: 1).

In order to minimize the itching and scratching (and thus avoid any rash), treatment is similar to that used with hives—the application of soothing lotions and creams or taking baths. In more severe cases, cortisone, tranquilizers, and antihistamines may be indicated. Should it be impossible to eliminate the cause completely, immunization or desensitization are necessary, especially in those instances where hay fever or asthma symptoms are present. The process of desensitization is harmless and is accomplished by injecting small amounts of the allergen until immunity is achieved and no further unfavorable reactions occur. The amounts are increased very slowly and are always administered with expert medical supervision.

Millie

For a long time, Millie frustrated everyone who tried to help her. Physically, she suffered from severe dermatitis. During early childhood, she endured annual sieges of blisters that covered most of her body for a month and then left it dry and scaly. Added to her misery were frequent attacks of asthma. By the time Millie reached adolesence, she had already manifested psychological symptoms that were obviously related to her painful childhood years. She was often deeply depressed and used the excuse of constant weariness to avoid attendance at school and rehabilitation counseling sessions or even meeting friends. Her physical symptoms seemed to warrant little cause for optimism. Although she suffered no recurrence of asthma and her dermatitis returned every two or three years now instead of annually, the attacks were of greater duration, as long as three or four months. At these times, her skin was red, her hands scaly and warty, and she exuded a disagreeable odor.

Millie and her rehabilitation counselors knew that her condition was chronic and that her chances for a complete cure were poor. But despite Millie's self-defeating attempts—sometimes retreating inward, sometimes bursting into hostility—her rehabilitation counselors persisted. Their advantage lay in her essential insight into her own personality and her residual inner determination. It was gratifying to hear her admit at last (she was seventeen at this point) that she had not given up hope entirely. "You know," she said, "it might improve with age. My grandmother used to have it even worse than me, but after she got married, she got better and better."

As treatments with ultraviolet light and hormones began to help, Millie began to talk about preparing for a vocation—the direction in which her counselors had patiently tried to guide her. Since she had shown a desire to work, possessed an average intelligence and a pleasant voice, the counselors hinted at telephone training. Progress was, however, agonizingly slow. Still anxious and self-conscious about her appearance, she frequently withdrew and sulked silently for several days. But always she came back, eager to learn more about herself in therapy, to absorb reassurance that she could salvage her life.

Counseling helped her to release also her long-suppressed feelings of anger and hostility toward an overpowering mother. That step forward was hesitant, too, and not without accompanying unpleasantness. When she manifested strong emotion, her mother lashed back, as Millie reported, "Ever since you went for help, you get worse, not better. And who ends up taking care of you, as usual?" Guilt-ridden with self-accusations of ingratitude, Millie would again retreat into herself, and another outcropping of blisters would appear. The happy intervention of the family doctor helped enormously, for he was able to offer Millie encouragement in her quest for independence and, even more important at this critical stage, to assure her mother that Millie was not an invalid and was wholly capable of living a useful and reasonably happy life. Most significant of all, he convinced them both that many of Millie's recurrent skin problems were directly related to emotional factors such as anxiety and tension induced by family pressure.

In time, Millie trained with the telephone company and was hired as a switchboard operator. Her dermatitis was not completely cured, but she suffered fewer attacks and those were considerably less severe.

HAY FEVER AND ALLERGIC RHINITIS

Hay fever, the most common of all allergies, cannot be casually dismissed as a minor nuisance, least of all by the close to 13 million Americans who start sneezing en masse every year. The hay fever sufferer endures many miseries: he is frequently unable to continue with his normal activities, loses many working days, feels exhausted and irritable much of the time, and may have frequent colds and sustain high expense for medicine and doctor's visits. Infections of the nose, eyes, ears, throat, and sinuses are not uncommon, nor are polyps that cluster in the nose and sinuses and ultimately have to be removed surgically. True, mild cases are no cause for alarm, but the consequences of not treating or controlling severe cases of hay fever can be significant. The hay fever victim—who has already inherited a tendency toward this allergy—is in constant danger of developing far more serious complications. Several reports state that one out of every three hay fever patients may develop asthma, a serious ailment, which can lead to permanent damage of the lungs and heart.

The ancients believed that the nose was a holy organ and that sneezing was a holy symbol as one's soul departed the body by way of the nose (McGovern and Knight 1957: x). But superstition affords little comfort when one's eyes are swollen, red, watery, burning and itching, or when one's clogged nose is incessantly running midst recurrent seizures of sneezing and coughing. We need only observe a full-fledged hay fever attack to understand why many victims would do almost anything to escape the sometimes violent symptoms of hay fever. Some sufferers develop sinus headaches from the swelling of the nasal membranes. Blocked nasal passages compel others to breathe through their mouths. Still others develop itching of the mouth, throat, or ear canals, and, in instances when the bronchial tubes become affected from the inhaled pollen, coughing and labored breathing result. In sum, hay fever is not called the king of the allergies for nothing. Unhappily, it is a tyranny whose subjects have legitimate cause for tears, depression, and exhaustion.

In early nineteenth-century England, hay was falsely considered to be the cause of hay fever. Today we know that the primary cause is inhalation of pollen. Although ragweed is the main culprit in the United States, there are, in addition to weeds, two other pollinating agents—trees and grasses. These airborne pollens are as abundant as they are tiny and almost weightless. Pollen has been found as far as 400 miles from its source and as high as 1,700 feet above sea level. (Other causes of hay fever, more recently recognized, include mold spores and insect dust.) Hay fever symptoms do not occur in the first year of life or during the first year of exposure to the offending pollens. Sometimes it takes months or years for the body to manufacture enough sensitizing antibodies which, when combined with the pollen, mold, dust, and the like produce the familiar hay fever reactions.

Because the plants that disperse hay fever pollen vary in potency not only from season to season but from place to place, it is difficult to predict who will become a victim and when or where the allergy will strike. Moreover, people vary considerably in their sensitivity to certain allergens. Thus the severity of any given case of hay fever commonly depends upon such variables as the amount of pollen in the air, the person's degree of sensitivity, where he lives, and temperature and barometric changes in a particular season. Spring hay fever is mostly caused by pollen from elm, maple, birch, and other common trees, whereas midsummer hay fever is generally a result of pollinating grasses. The most offensive and virulent type, however, is the ragweed pollen that precipitates mid-August hay fever attacks. Knowledge of these offenders and their pollinating seasons gives hay fever patients a better chance to identify their particular sensitivity and have their symptoms treated. Any person suffering enough to consider a change in residence will wisely consult his doctor or the Ragweed Pollen Index issued by the Pollen Survey Committee of the American Academy of Allergy for local areas in North America where the environment will prove least offensive to his particular allergy *(Hay Fever* 1966*)*.

For those less extremely affected, there are, nonetheless, other environmental hazards to confront. Damp, cold, and fog intensify distress for some hay fever sufferers; warmth, heat, and dry or sunny climate do the same for others. Strong odors, animal hairs, house dust, and even certain foods exacerbate the condition. Each of these stimuli is an indirect cause of irritation, working cumulatively in combination with a specific pollen to increase sensitivity. Yet another secondary cause has been cited by analytically oriented doctors whose patients manifest symptoms akin to hay fever but seem, in fact, to be victims of emotional disturbance—especially fear, grief, anguish, humiliation, and resentment (Harris and Shure 1969: 155). Though most doctors acknowledge that emotions may aggravate basic allergic conditions, no one has yet demonstrated that emotion is a direct cause of hay fever—or any other allergy.

Diagnosis of hay fever is relatively simple: detailed history of symptoms and their characteristic traits, time of onset, skin tests, and the like. Furthermore, the condition of the nose with its "gray, boggy, swollen membrane and large amounts of water secretion" (Harris and Shure 1969: 155) helps differentiate symptoms of hay fever from those of the common cold with its accompanying sore throat, temperature, nose stuffed by a thick secretion that dries up and crusts over. Another condition, known as *perennial allergic rhinitis,* or *year-round hay fever,* has similar symptons and is treated in the same way as seasonal hay fever. But allergic rhinitis (once known as *sinus* or *catarrh* or *summer cold*) is caused by inhalation of indoor substances—dust, feathers, bacterial infections, foods, wool, animal hairs, cottons, and the molds and mildew of household objects. The persistent irritation caused by year-round hay fever is likely to produce polyps and infection of the sinuses, and may also result in temporary loss of taste and smell.

What, then, should be done when an adolescent shows symptoms of hay fever? First of all, he or his parents, teachers, or counselor should insist upon immediate consultation with a physician. A reasonable youth will quickly understand the risks of haphazard self-medication if he does have hay fever. He may be less easy about giving up his favorite feather pillow or a food to which he has been unknowingly allergic. Although a girl may be delighted that she no longer has to dust the furniture, she may balk at giving up her cat or switching to allergy-free cosmetics. But these precautions, both youths must learn, are necessary not only to their physical comfort but also to their psychic well-being. It is the task of the doctor, parent, and counselor to guide the adolescent toward the decision he must make for his own welfare.

BRONCHIAL ASTHMA

In the United States 12,600,000 people a year (or 6 percent of the population) live through asthma attacks.

This number represents more than the combined total of those suffering multiple sclerosis, cerebral palsy, polio, and arthritis. Five million of these asthmatic patients are permanently incapacitated from bronchial asthma and cannot continue with normal school, employment, or household chores. Others find that the least amount of exertion leaves them gasping for breath or choking. They too must drastically limit their range of activity. Curiously, few asthma victims regard their affliction as serious or dangerous enough to warrant professional attention. Perhaps, those who suffer this malady have wrongly assumed that because they have lived with it since childhood, nothing can be done. But though it is generally accepted that all asthma may be traced to the early years (usually before the age of five—and many allergists argue that a natural progression ensues from infantile eczema to hay fever and finally to asthma), it is foolish and self-destructive to accept this kind of suffering by remaining ignorant of palliative measures.

Asthma means literally "to gasp for breath." Many other conditions have asthmatic symptoms (labored breathing, coughing, and wheezing). Here we are concerned with the disease, bronchial asthma, caused by allergy resulting in an obstruction of the passage of air through the lungs. That impediment to breathing may be due to one of several malfunctions: swelling of the membranes of the bronchial tubes; contraction of muscles around the tubes; or a blockage of the small bronchial tubes by thickened mucus (*Handbook for the Asthmatic* 1966: 1-15). Since these symptoms are allergic in origin, the familiar antigen-antibody reaction has already taken place in the bronchial tract—the shock organ—before the appearance of an asthma attack.

Violent as hay fever symptoms may be, they do not compare to the terror and suffering of an asthmatic attack. Yet much of the helplessness and fear of suffocation or dying that victims know during an attack could be substantially alleviated if they were aware that the asthma attack itself is seldom as serious or dangerous as it looks or feels. Relief is available and peace of mind possible if only sufferers will learn the facts about their disease and take the steps necessary to control it. However tedious and time consuming, all the tests and examinations required to determine the cause of their allergy must be undertaken. Early detection and treatment are crucial.

The most common type of bronchial asthma is caused by nonliving allergens (pollen, mold, antibiotics, certain foods, and so on). Other causes are also possible: respiratory, viral, and bacterial infections and some cardiac conditions (mostly with older adults). In all instances, however, the symptoms are the same and follow the usual allergic mechanism—the cause alone differs. Cause, symptoms, severity, and conditions surrounding this disease vary from patient to patient. One may cough persistently, run short of breath, yet not wheeze. His attacks may be brief, occur infrequently, and he may even be, for long periods of time, completely free of symptoms. (During this remission the presence of asthma can be detected only by specific tests.) Others, less fortunate, may have daily attacks with no periods of respite, yet show no sign of a cough. One person's attack may be precipitated by a specific substance, say, the family cat. How simple. Remove the cause, relieve the asthma. If it worked, this would be considered a mild case of asthma, even though the symptoms were dramatic and violent. It is not likely, however, that all cats can be eliminated any more than it is feasible to eradicate all the pollen or molds that cause asthma. But if the symptoms respond satisfactorily to medication taken by mouth or inhalation or when the specific antigen is removed or avoided, the chances are overwhelming that the asthma is a mild case.

If relief is not obtained that readily, immunization or desensitization treatments are called for. Desensitization treatments, doctors report (Harris and Shure 1969: 181), have lasting effect for about 80 percent of the people who take them, whereas 10 percent may have to return in a few years for booster shots, and another 10 percent may need injections for the rest of their lives. A new, one-shot repository treatment is still in the experimental stage. Interestingly, although the underlying allergic process is similar here to that in all other allergies, antihistamines are not in the least bit helpful—instead, they can actually make matters worse. The object in symptomatic treatment for asthma is to stop the spasm of the bronchial muscles, decrease the swelling of the membranes, and thin the sticky mucus. Antihistamine, on the other hand, may actually increase the obstruction by causing a drying and hardening of the mucus. Epinephrein (injection or inhalation), isoproternol (inhalation), and ephedrine and theophylline (oral) all offer relief from asthma attacks. Other preparations may be given rectally. Iodide of potassium and glycerol guiacolate, lots of water, and inhalation of steam are recommended to loosen and thin heavy mucus. And, the newer cortisone remedies are very effective for more severe cases. Cortisone remedies, however, require close medical supervision because of the possibility of serious side effects (Harris and Shure 1969: 205).

Instructions in how to breathe properly—especially how to exhale—during an asthma attack can be helpful for those who have severe cases. Many people believe erroneously that the trouble is a lack of oxygen. In fact, the patient has enough oxygen, but he can't get it into his lungs. Under instruction, the patient is first taught how to relax and then, by demonstration, how he can control his breathing and not suffocate during an attack. As he uses his diaphragm and abdominal and chest muscles correctly, he learns how to empty his lungs with every exhalation to make room for fresh air.

People who have asthma should maintain good physical health and neither smoke nor drink alcohol. They should avoid strong cooking odors, fumes, sudden temperature changes, colds, and dampness. They should treat infections promptly and enjoy plenty of rest. As much as possible, they should keep free from emotional strain and anxiety.

Chronic cases of asthma are more likely to develop complications. Over a long period of time, damage to the small air sacs in the lungs eventually occurs, and they lose their ability to snap back. As the smaller air sacs fuse with one another to form larger air sacs, the stagnant air is not completely exhaled, and infections develop more readily. Some doctors believe that these are the conditions that most readily lead to the development of emphysema, the most *serious* complication of asthma. Other complications include collapsed lungs, chronic bronchitis, heart strain, and emotional difficulties. All may develop if the cause of the allergy is not detected, treated, or eliminated. But insofar as any of these complications involves breathing, it is always possible—if the allergic cause can be discovered and treated before permanent damage to the elasticity of the membranes occurs—to halt deterioration and reverse the trend. In other words, bronchial asthma can be not only treated but also cured.

On very rare occasions, *status asthmaticus* or *intractable asthma* may develop. Both are extreme, persistent forms of asthma that resist treatment and require hospitalization, intravenous therapy, or inhalation treatment. Sometimes, the doctor can remove the thick plugs that are blocking the airways or use pressure breathing machines (IPPB). Surgical interference has not proved to be very successful as treatment for these rare but severe forms of bronchial asthma. With modern techniques and medicine, however, such severe complications of asthma occur infrequently. Nevertheless, the occasional fatality is a grim reminder of the seriousness of the disease and of the inescapable importance of a rigorous and unswerving commitment to treatment after early detection.

Hippocrates documented the emotional component of asthma when he warned that "the asthmatic must guard against anger" (McGovern and Knight 1957: V). Nevertheless, the study of psychological influences upon asthma is relatively new. Few physicians deny the impact of psychological problems upon the asthmatic condition itself, but practically all warn against attributing the cause of the disease solely to tension, anxiety, and emotional conflict (Newman 1963: 434). The case history given here illustrates the medical realities of the situation but points up as well the relevance of psychological awareness on the part of patient, parent, counselor, and physician.

Dennis

Dennis seemed to be a well-adjusted, happy teenager. He had friends but preferred to remain alone most of the time and to give his time to his hobbies—body building, astronomy, and medicine. He was an only son whose father had left home when he was six and whose mother had, as head of the family, worked as a nurse. Although Dennis had had asthma since infancy, his attacks became progressively worse after his father's death and soon resisted almost all treatment. Nevertheless, Dennis' mother, a capable, intelligent, sensitive woman, tried hard to avoid, as she said, "babying Dennis just because he was only a child and without a father." Her insight and effort were not entirely in vain. On the surface, at least, Dennis showed evidence of a healthy quest after independence, and his mother deferred as often as possible to her son, letting him make his own decisions.

Yet an undercurrent of ambivalence coursed through their relationship. Further observation and investigation made clear that Dennis was, in fact, a shy and lonely youth who had barely managed to control his depression. His emotional and social development had been arrested despite his confident, ambitious assertions: "I'm going to prepare for med school, marry, and have three children." Psychological testing revealed also his overwhelming feelings of helplessness for which he compensated by daydreams of success and achievement. Beneath his self-assured proclamations, Dennis fretted and worried like any other adolescent—only more so. He doubted his masculinity but denied any interest in sex; he avoided peer companionship; and he tried to overcome his physical weakness by adhering to a strict body-building regime.

On an even deeper level of consciousness, he thought of himself as a sickly child, unable to care for himself and terrified that his mother would abandon him just as his father had years earlier. In order not to lose his mother —toward whom he harbored unconscious aggressive and hostile feelings—and to assure himself of her love and approval, he tried bravely to be what she wished: independent, mature, and confident. Try as he might, however, Dennis could not rid himself of deeply rooted feelings developed and manifest when he was a small child—feelings of complete helplessness, of fear of dying during an asthmatic attack, and of total dependence upon his mother.

Here, then, is a classic example of how a psychological imbalance may aggravate the difficulties of an asthmatic youth. A study of the timing and intensity of his attacks suggested that they were closely related to his inward turmoil and fears. *When* Dennis suffered an attack had something to do with his emotional reaction to a particular experience. But Dennis and his mother were both determined to battle against his suffering. For the next two years, he stayed at a special hospital, where he received both physical and psychological care. His physical symptoms gradually responded to special diet and reduced steroid medication. At the same time, Dennis worked with a male psychotherapist whom he liked and trusted. He began for the first time to recognize and express his infantile fears of separation and rejection. Encouraged by a diminution in the number of his attacks while he was in therapy, Dennis seemed willing to talk about his fears more freely. With guidance, he gained insight into how his asthma attacks had become a convenient means of binding him and his mother together and helping him to evade his real problems.

Setbacks did occur. Once he understood that by hiding behind his asthmatic attacks, he was refusing to recognize his hostility toward his mother, Dennis felt guilt and manifested it alternately through denial or depression. For a time, his attacks grew more frequent and more intense. The pattern of pathology was frighteningly neat. But as therapy continued, what became most clear was that Dennis' allergy was less significant in his illness than his psychological difficulties. Dennis was not completely cured of his asthma, but since his two years at the hospital, he has enjoyed freedom from asthmatic symptoms for the longest period he has ever known.

Most of the psychological literature about asthma is written from the psychoanalytic frame of reference and is concerned primarily with the mother-child relationship (French et al. 1941: Parts I and II, 1ff.). Although most researchers agree that there is no single "asthmatic personality," a number of traits in the adolescent profile (Fink and Schneer 1963: 205–224) suggest a pattern that begins in childhood. Frequently, the primary conflict centers upon an unresolved dependence on the mother.[1] The asthmatic teenager may thus be immature, neurotic, insecure, and unable to express his hostility toward a dominating mother who had earlier threatened rejection and withdrawal of her love. The tug of war between dependence and independence may inform an anxiety that manifests itself in the all-too-familiar somatic reaction—an attack of asthma.

Bronchial asthma is considered a classical psychosomatic disorder that often responds to psychotherapy (Kleeman 1967: 611–19). Therapeutic progress may be slow, however, and there may be considerable need also to help the parents with their problems while continuing to offer support and encouragement to the adolescent. No single form of psychotherapy can at this time be recommended as best. All we can safely affirm now is that therapy does, in many cases, alleviate symptoms (Feingold, Singer, Freeman, and Deskins 1966: 152–53).

NOTE

1. Fathers are also profoundly important in these circumstances, though less frequently as central as mothers. For a sensitive and discerning account of the father's role, see Abramson 1969.

REFERENCES

Abramson, Harold A., *Psychological Problems in the Father-Son Relationship: A Case of Eczema and Asthma*, New York, October House, 1969.

Feinberg, Samuel M., *Living with Your Allergy*, Philadelphia, J. B. Lippincott, 1968.

Feingold, Ben F., Margaret Thaler Singer, Edith H. Freeman, and Andrew Deskins, "Psychological Variables in Allergic Disease: A Critical Appraisal of Methodology," *Journal of Allergy 37* (Sept. 1966): 152–53.

Fink, Geraldine, and Henry I. Schneer, "Psychiatric Evaluation of Adolescent Asthmatics," in *The Asthmatic Child*, Henry I. Schneer, ed., New York, Harper and Row, 1963: 205–24.

French, T. M., et al, "Psychogenic Factors in Bronchial Asthma,"

Psychosomatic Medicine Monographs, Parts I and II, Washington, D. C., National Research Council, 1941.

Handbook for the Asthmatic, New York, Allergy Foundation of America, 1966.

Harris, M. Coleman, and Norman Shure, *All About Allergy,* Englewood Cliffs, N.J., Prentice-Hall, 1969.

Hay Fever . . . and What You Can Do About It, rev. ed., New York, Allergy Foundation of America, 1966.

Kleeman, Susan T., "Psychiatric Contributions in the Treatment of Asthma," *Annals of Allergy* 25 (1967): 611–19.

McGovern, John P., and James A. Knight, *Allergy and Human Emotion,* Springfield, Ill., Charles C Thomas, 1957.

Newman, Joseph, "Psychological Problems of Children and Youth with Chronic Medical Disorders," in *Psychology of Exceptional Children and Youth,* 2d ed., William M. Cruickshank, ed., Englewood Cliffs, N.J., Prentice-Hall, 1963: 394–447.

Skin and Its Allergies, The, New York, Allergy Foundation of America, 1966.

6

Brain Injury

Some physical handicaps yield readily to clinical diagnosis; others resist almost all efforts at classification. Few have been so stubborn as brain injury, whose seemingly infinite variations have all but fragmented the diagnostic pattern. Yet some hints of a shaping form have become discernible within the past twenty years. Although it is but a beginning, we are now beyond that time when, in brutal ignorance, a brain-injured person might be casually dismissed as an "odd-ball." With nearly forty descriptive terms[1] now in use, we have approached a consensus about who the brain-injured person is, what his needs are, and how he may best be helped. Estimates suggest that more than a million and a half school children in the United States (about 5 percent) are brain-injured, far too many of them still undiagnosed or, worse, incorrectly diagnosed[2]. Some of them are ignored or overlooked because their impairment is slight or barely discernible. In every entering class, one authority suggests, there may be one or two brain-injured children.

Until recent years, brain injury was a catch-all category for any chronic brain dysfunction, including major motor deficiencies like cerebral palsy and epilepsy or severe intellectual deficiency like mental retardation[3]. As it is used in this chapter, however (and this usage now has broad acceptance), brain injury applies only to minimal brain dysfunction with accompanying learning difficulties and behavioral problems.[4] Once we understand the special problems of the brain-injured child in relation to what we know about the normal sequence of growth and learning, we will be able to help him resolve those difficulties that would otherwise scar his adolescence and impede his adjustment to adult life.

We must begin with certain salient physiological truths. Because the brain functions as a whole, damage to any area of the brain always affects and alters the entire cerebral pattern. Depending upon the site and severity of the injury or the type of damage (tumor, hemorrhage, inflammation, and the like), behavior may be altered throughout the range of experience. Since brain injury may occur before, during, or after birth, the age at which an injury is sustained may also prove crucial. A relatively minor lesion in a vital area may result in a catastrophic alteration of performance, whereas demonstrably massive damage in a subordinate locale may educe no significant behavioral problems or learning difficulties.

The causes of injury may be organic or environmental: blood factors, the mother's health during pregnancy, difficult labor, lack of oxygen, severe childhood illnesses, infection, or head injury. Therefore, efforts at prevention focus on pregnancy, delivery, and early child care. Nevertheless, the brain damage cannot always be detected physiologically, and often the brain-injured child cannot be convincingly identified until he manifests socially unacceptable behavior or develops learning problems.

Diagnosis and treatment of the brain-injured person should include the services of a neurologist, a psychiatrist, a psychologist, and a special educator. Often specialized skills may be needed also: an ophthalmologist (for vision), an otologist (for hearing),[5] and a language and speech therapist. Why so many specialists? Simply because the spectrum of problems is so wide, including myriad learning and behavioral abnormalities—poor coordination, sensory impairment, and speech and language disorders—that there is a real need for a more comprehensive examination and evaluation by different disciplines. Moreover, although this handicap is basically neurological, a diagnosis of brain injury is not always definitive on the basis of neurological tests alone. The EEG (electroencephalogram), as well as other neurological techniques, frequently does not reveal either the presence or the cause of cerebral dysfunction. The neurologist, therefore, looks for other so-called soft signs, or developmental irregularities, which may suggest brain damage: irregular rhythms of speech and breathing, awkward gait, poor eye-hand coordination, more strength in one arm, or inappropriate gestures and facial expressions. Other motor and postural tests may likewise indicate the presence of cerebral disease. A medical history including details about pregnancy, delivery, childhood diseases, high fevers, convulsions, concussion, or other accidents also helps in some instances to establish the etiology of brain injury. In any event, medical reports and all diagnostic evaluations should be simply stated and usefully related to treatment.

On occasion, it is the psychiatrist who can best discriminate the subtly overlapping psychological and/or physiological symptoms and thus differentiate the mentally retarded or the emotionally disturbed from the brain-injured. Psychological tests too may verify the diagnosis of brain injury and contribute appreciably to learning and behavioral evaluations. For example, a number of tests[6] highlight conspicuous signs of organic defects: much lower scores on nonverbal (performance) tests than on verbal tests; obvious distortions in the areas of vision, hearing, or motor coordination; significant defects in memory, or marked difficulty in organizational or planning skills.

Medical, psychiatric, and psychological tests should not be relied upon as the sole basis for diagnosis. Special educators, for example, may more readily recognize specific discrepancies in perceptual or motor development sequences that may aid the classroom teacher in isolating and identifying the brain-injured child's specific developmental lags—sensory, motor, or language maturational processes. Thus it is most important to determine a child's central disability (e.g., visual perceptual impairment) and to identify as well any relevant secondary characteristic (e.g., some motor coordination difficulties). All diagnoses and evaluations, then, should aim toward an honest, realistic estimate of how far the patient can be educated and how well he can be prepared to care for himself physically, psychologically, socially, and vocationally.

The challenge is great, the task less than simple. Knowledge about brain injury is too far ahead of the facilities needed for diagnosis, treatment, and education. Even if a patient is accurately diagnosed, uncertainty and confusion attend upon how and where he may be helped. The problem is complicated by the inescapable need for individualized treatment and education. Medically, for example, some patients respond to the use of sedatives (phenobarbital), others to anti-convulsant drugs (dilantin), and still others to stimulants (amphetamines, ritalin). In education, special elementary classes for the brain-injured child have only recently been established (since 1955, New York State has established ninety) and they are too few to service the needs of the brain-injured adolescent. But the brain-injured child is able to learn. He cannot be taught by the methods used with normal children or by those used to teach the deaf, the blind, or the mentally retarded. However difficult it may be to diagnose, treat, or educate him, the fact remains that diagnosis, treatment, and education are possible and, for the sake of each of these children and their society, necessary.

Although more than one hundred symptoms have
been identified, they fall conveniently into two major
groupings—learning difficulties and behavioral disorders. To separate and investigate each of these aspects of
our total mental apparatus may seem arbitrary but need
not do disservice to the concept of the total personality.
Instead, it may enrich our understanding of how the
brain-injured patient functions in his environment, how
his disability affects his performance at different times,
in different situations, and under different conditions.
Furthermore, this approach may help us to recognize
that what were formerly considered as isolable defects
are merely modified symptoms of the same brain damage.

Learning is an exceedingly complicated process involving all our sensory responses. In orderly fashion, it
proceeds from perception: simple observation (which includes seeing, hearing, tasting, touching, and smelling)
of objects, persons, and situations, to conception: abstract thinking, or the organization of percepts into systems of knowledge to behavior: purposeful activity. Inte-
grally related to the normal process of learning are
developmental patterns of speech and language. These
processes—percepts, concepts, language, and behavior—
continuously interact, modifying one another to affect
nearly all our responses to experience. Aware that there
are no separate organs of perception, conception, or language, we may more readily understand the complex
integrating functions of the brain. Although we see with
our eyes and hear with our ears, we are dependent upon
a less tangible yet more complex neuropsychic system in

the brain to modify these impressions to assure a sequence of adequate learning and appropriate behavior.
All our sensory experiences follow the same sequence:
registering impressions on the brain (perception), organ-
izing and integrating them (conception). Only through
this causal sequence does a normal pattern of action
(behavior) ensue.

Learning and behavior patterns in the brain-injured
child, however, are crucially disrupted because of basic
disturbances in the perceptive-conceptual processes that
have also created difficulties with his speech and language development. Let us for a few moments use a
simple example to dramatize the distortions that mark
the perceptions and conceptions of the brain-injured
child when they are contrasted with those of a normal
person.

A normal spectator usually marvels at the architec-
tural splendor and esthetic beauty of the Leaning Tower
of Pisa and, incidentally, may also relish watching tour-
ists mount or descend its spiral ramp. But a brain-
injured child may suddenly point excitedly to a footsore
tourist carrying her shoes as she walks along the ramp
and ask, "Why is she wearing her shoes on her hand?"
or "Where did the steps go?" Normally, we perceive an
object or scene all at once and as a whole; we fix "the
picture" firmly in our minds. Not so for the perceptually
deficient. Unable to grasp the whole, he rarely gets "the
picture," but tends rather to perceive insignificant or
trivial details. He becomes fixed upon a part of the whole
and may even shift too readily to other parts as well.
Little wonder, then, that characteristics such as inattention, distractibility, poor concentration, and distorted
sense of reality are attributed to him.

A well-meaning but misguided parent might persist in efforts at cultural enrichment and even derive satisfaction when the brain-injured child exclaims, "Why is that building falling?" But the child may not have grasped at all the significance or uniqueness of the tower and have responded merely from an early developmental level of thinking (animism) in which an inanimate object (the tower) is endowed with lifelike qualities (falling). The parent's pleasure is likely to be short-lived when the questions are asked again about the lady's shoes, where the steps went, or new and equally disturbing comments are made, such as, "That isn't a tower; the Empire State is the tower."

What lies behind these responses? The trouble begins at the level of perception. A normal person perceives in terms of figure and ground (background). The brain-injured has difficulty in establishing such relationships, frequently reversing the two so that the barefoot lady becomes the figure, the tower the minor detail, or ground. Moreover, perhaps because of excitement, the pressure of parental expectation, feelings of opposition, anxiety, frustration, or inadequacy, the brain-injured child may perseverate in thought, speech, or action, that is, automatically repeat his responses beyond necessary or appropriate limits.[7]

The brain-injured child's perceptually distorted image of the Leaning Tower of Pisa makes inevitable distortions of conception as well, distortions of the abstract or generalized thinking that follows perception. In a normal sequence, perception is the process between seeing and thinking whereby objects and people (external sensory stimuli) are registered and ordered by the brain (the lady, the steps, the tower). Further organization, gener-

alization, and reshaping of these impressions into abstractions and formulas for decision or action are functions of the conceptual process. Thus, the parent automatically sees the relationship and similarity of the
Pisan tower to other buildings; he can generalize from
past experiences and learning; and he can recognize the
artistic and historical significance of the tower by virtue
of symbolic images and memories. But his brain-injured
child can do none of these things. Lacking the capacity
to abstract, he cannot generalize to another kind of tower
in another place at another time. Granted that the child
lacks a wide range of experience upon which to draw, he
is none the less locked within a rigid, incomplete, distorted, concretized perceptual-conceptual pattern. It is
impossible for him to mean the same thing when he says
"I see" and "I understand," statements the normal person makes with assurance.

Perceptual deficiencies inevitably interfere with the
accuracy of the images the brain-injured child acquires
and naturally inhibit his manipulating abstractions into
mature and sophisticated mental constructs. This self-
perpetuating tendency to repeat earlier developmental
distortions is another characteristic of the brain-injured
child. One of the first remedial stages must direct itself
toward correcting faulty new perceptions to forestall a
destructive reliance upon already established false perceptions and conceptions (Goldstein 1959; Bender 1956:
3, 52). One may ask, for example, what kind of memory
the brain-injured child has. If he remembers the tower
atop the Empire State Building in New York, which he
has visited on many occasions, why can he not recall
explanations recently given in answer to his persistent

questions? We may reason that particular details remain
in his memory for a longer time because he is unable to
generalize; they fail to merge with other details or fade
into the background of more complex patterns. On the
other hand, his perceptual instability and limited success
in shaping concepts leave fewer traces (memories) for
him to recall. Related to this problem is the apparent
contradiction between perseveration and distractibility.
At times, he appears to be stuck with a single detail, or
he drifts from one detail to another, giving alternate
impressions of perseveration, and distraction and a continuing effect of inconsistency. The common denomina-
tor here may be the brain-injured child's inadequate control of his images, ideas, or actions, enabling them to
disappear completely or to remain and be continuously
rehearsed.

An experienced observer watching a brain-injured
youngster trying to play basketball will recognize several other practices that distinguish, and in this case
segregate, him from others: he can't understand or follow the rules of the game (conceptualizations); he is
poorly coordinated; and he is an exceedingly poor judge
of size, shape, distance or direction. Since basketball depends upon coordination of perceptual and motor functions, he is at a disadvantage. Unsure of his own body
and its parts in relationship to himself and to his environment, he can't aim or catch the ball, or tell where the
basket is in relation to himself or the ball. Perhaps with
special training, he may master the more basic skills. But
then he must deal with players of two teams who chase
after each other and the ball, constantly shifting positions. It is not unusual for the brain-injured player to

confuse members of his team with the opposition. Intent
upon guarding his man, his attention may switch suddenly to other players running down the court, and he
may innocently join in the chase. Furthermore, he has
considerable difficulty not tripping over his own feet or
crashing into running players. The situation is not likely
to endear the brain-injured player to his teammates. To
them he is clumsy, awkward, or stupid. His peers are
frankly impatient with him and not at all reluctant to tell
him so. An unwelcome member of the team, he is dis-
placed, lost, unable to find his place in the scheme of
things. His behavior is as unacceptable to his peers as it
is to adults. Dejected and rejected, he sinks into even
more disorganized and purposeless behavior. Burdened
from the outset with an extremely low frustration level,
he may impulsively and belligerently defend himself.
Unable to assess the consequences of such unruly, dis-
ruptive, often wild behavior, he is thrown out of the
game. The brain-injured child's difficulty in establishing
cause and effect relationships, as well as his inability to
organize experiences, renders him equally incapable of
making practical or realistic predictions.[8]

If we add to these examples the range of possibility
opened by failures in other sense impressions registered
upon a defective sensory-motor system, our awareness of
the brain-injured child's bewilderment with the world
should become real. It is only mildly reassuring to know
that any given brain-injured child rarely manifests more
than two or three of the major characteristics of the
illness. Denied to him are our comfortably inherent
sense of order and our predictably purposeful behavior,
even in a chaotic, ever-changing world. For him—at least

until we redirect him—there is only change, chaos, disorganization, and disorientation.

Yet another area in which research has only recently begun to further understanding of both normal and brain-injured adolescents is the study of body-image. Body-image, basically a psychological phenomenon, is the mental picture that every individual has of his body, regardless of how closely the image resembles his actual appearance.[9] During adolescence, all youths—the brain-damaged and normal alike—undergo abrupt and radical physical changes as well as increased social and emotional pressures. These are the years when the body-image takes on new significance, particularly in terms of the impression one makes on others and how one views his own body. At this time of flux, the adolescent is extraordinarily sensitive to his concept of himself as intensely responsive to parental attitudes and values, to his sexual development, to his peer status, and to the discrepancy between his real and ideal body-images. Although the personality is essentially formed during childhood, a reshuffling and reintegration occur during adolescence, at which time self-esteem and senses of independence and security are re-evaluated. Academic and vocational decisions help to precipitate a realistic examination of abilities, aspirations, and values. These and like stimuli affect the delicate balance between a healthy, well-integrated ego supported by a realistic body-image and a maladjusted, inadequate ego weakened by a distorted body-image.

Not all normal adolescents, even those with uneven maturational processes, experience disturbed body-images. On the other hand, some teenagers within the normal range of development may experience marked distortion of their body-image. Among the brain-injured, however, almost all suffer some body disorientation. The brain-injured adolescent has, and has always had, the same physical, emotional, and social needs as other children. His burden is particularly weighted during these crucial years by his distorted body-image—another consequence of his specific organic and perceptual-conceptual irregularities. The brain-injured child's distorted body image, then, must be seen as directly related to his brain injury. Only when we have this understanding can we help him toward a more realistic yet affirmative body-image of himself.

Richie

Let us now consider the experiences of some brain-injured youngsters who have tried—necessarily through their distorted sensorium—to adapt to the world. In the first account, the mother of Richie, a sixteen-year-old, brain-injured adolescent, details the misunderstanding, misinformation, and mistreatment encountered in her search for advice and help. There follows an examination of Richie's earlier records—educational, medical, and psychiatric. Finally, we note his progress after two years of special training.

"I had trouble with Richie as soon as he started school —all complaints, no help. I was told, 'He never sits still, he's perpetual motion, always fidgety, nervous, and won't pay attention.' At home, he acted like a big baby and was very stubborn. Even today, if he doesn't get his way, we can expect a temper tantrum but nothing like before. Anyway, the school finally sent me to a psychiatrist, who said he had 'emotional problems,' and Richie went for treatment once every week for a year. But there was no change in school or at home. He refused to study; he couldn't keep up with the other children; he couldn't get along with boys or girls his age; and they told me I would have to take him out and put him in an institution. My husband wouldn't let me. He said, 'There's nothing wrong with the boy, he will outgrow it.'

"So we sent him to a private school for slow learners and they told me he was 'mentally retarded' and we shouldn't expect him to learn like normal children. So we left him alone—he never did his homework, he never did what he was told. He acted like a clown, always avoided an issue and tried to make everyone laugh. He was tricky, though; I didn't believe he was really that stupid. Some things he could do all right when he wanted to, and he could always figure out how to make money. He would collect empty bottles or make deliveries for the drug store or grocery store in our neighborhood.

"Then one day, when he was about fourteen years old, he got hit in the head and we thought he had a concussion. The hospital took x rays and other tests, and told us he was 'brain damaged,' not mentally retarded or emotionally disturbed, and that he belonged in a different school where they would teach him how to learn.

"I don't know. He's still not like other children, but he's better than he was. At least he is learning for the past two years at the school he is at, and the teacher and the psychiatrist there have helped me understand how to handle him better."

Richie's diagnosis had indeed been altered several times during his sixteen years. A close review of his school records showed that in kindergarten and first grade his teachers reported: "Poor coordination—he cannot fasten his clothes, tie his shoelaces or run very well. He has difficulty holding a pencil, he does not have clear right-hand dominance, he cannot draw or print well and his speech is poor." Richie's teachers, his mother noted, told her: "His behavior is incorrigible. He has to be supervised constantly and restrained from destroying school property and hitting the other children."[10] Nevertheless, Richie had no difficulty learning to read or understanding simple number concepts. By the second and third grade, however, his behavior was reported as "unmanageable in the classroom." Furthermore, he was no longer working at the same academic grade level as his classmates. He was a poor reader and speller and had difficulty with arithmetic. A history of "learning difficulties and behavior problem" had—from the point of view of the school authorities—been adequately established.

Richie's medical history recorded a normal delivery, the usual childhood diseases but high fevers of about 103° to 106° for about six months before his tonsils were removed at the age of six—the year he started school. At eight years of age a psychiatrist had diagnosed him as Childhood Schizophrenic. His behavior was described as "inappropriate, bizarre, and unrealistic." A few years later, at ten, his IQ was noted as Borderline Defective; a neurological examination revealed "no cerebral dysfunction." He was placed in a class for the mentally retarded. The chance accident when he was fourteen, after hope had been abandoned, led to renewed effort and happier prospects for Richie's future. At that time a neurologist stated that the EEG showed a "pattern of underlying organic damage . . . cause undetermined."

Further psychiatric and clinical evidence indicated that Richie was an extremely lonesome, immature, and anxious adolescent boy with a history of socially maladaptive behavior and serious learning problems caused by minimal brain dysfunction. The diagnosis: Organic Brain Syndrome.[11] His intelligence was estimated as close to average potential, but the diagnosis added that effects of brain damage, subsequent emotional and behavioral problems, together with inadequate education, had combined to inhibit seriously the development of "undamaged" potential. A detailed analysis of Richie's perceptual and conceptual discrepancies located his major disability as visual. Not that his vision was poor. On the contrary, his sight was quite good. But the total system was blighted—the interlocking pattern of seeing, registering, interpreting, and remembering that he needed to respond appropriately and to learn effectively. An integrated educational and therapeutic program was recommended for Richie (and a special program for his parents) and he was placed in a special school. Richie's education began, not with reading, writing, and arithmetic, but with a program of sensory training, reorganization of the body, learning space relationships, and the like.

After two years of special training, Richie, now sixteen years old, underwent another battery of psychological tests to determine his progress. Intellectually, he now performed just below average, his report noting, however, a "strong likelihood that his intellectual level may continue to rise with further training." Language development, improvement in reading skills, more effective organization and integration of his thoughts and feelings —all had spurred Richie's intellectual growth. Emotionally, too, there were marked changes. His report indicated feelings of inferiority and an apprehension about his future that he tried to conceal on occasion by bragging: "I haven't decided what I want to be yet; probably a brain surgeon or something." But Richie had also become more amenable as a person, less aggressive than earlier reports had indicated. In part, this change might be the result of his age, smaller classes, reduced and controlled stimuli within his surroundings, and patient, sensitive, and specialized teachers. Together, all of these helped to work dramatic alterations in Richie's life, intellectually and emotionally.

Had Richie "outgrown" his problems, as his father predicted? Frequently, the overactive child does become less rambunctious and more pliant as he approaches adolescence, but this does not automatically guarantee that all his difficulties will vanish. Not until Richie was fourteen, and then only through a painful but lucky accident, was his condition belatedly identified as brain-injured. Thus, only after the correct diagnosis was established and Richie was placed in a proper setting that assured competent professional guidance did his parents learn what it means to be brain-injured: that to be brain-injured does not necessarily mean to be "mentally retarded" or "crazy." And only with hindsight did they understand Richie's confusing behavior and his fluctuating intellectual competency. They learned that inconsistency—a consequence of his uneven development—is typical of the brain-injured person (*not* so of the mentally retarded). Under a program of modified psychotherapy integrated with special educational personnel, his parents realized also that no matter what the diagnosis, Richie's emotional and physical needs were the same as those of other children. Despite his handicap, he need not have been spoiled, overprotected, or, on occasion, have had too much expected of him. Perhaps Richie's need to achieve success and self-respect was greater than others', especially because he had been deprived of the usual growth and progress that other children took for granted. It became clear to his parents too just how dependent Richie was upon both them and his teachers to help him become independent and to develop faith in his capacity to make the best possible adjustment to his disability. Above all, they learned that his difficulties would not simply vanish. Only the correction of Richie's basic deficiencies could prepare him for further education and training for a happier and more productive life.[12] Until such learning took place Richie's parents were powerless to help him or themselves.

Gary

Occasionally we meet a brain-injured person who is extremely quiet and passive (hypoactive or hypokinetic), not so overactive (hyperkinetic) as Richie was. Gary was overlooked because he hardly spoke, never caused argu-

ments, or had fights with the other children, and was
meticulously neat and orderly about his possessions and
his appearance. He seemed less than bright; in fact, he
was generally considered to be so dull that his slow progress in school surprised no one. Most children ignored
or taunted Gary. For a long time this did not seem to
bother him. He remained silent, impassive, apparently
unmoved. Among the children at play, Gary was always
the last to be chosen for a team. Finally, Gary refused to
play at all and usually watched from the sidelines. His
overt behavior posed no threat to others, but Gary's tendency toward excessive daydreams and fantasies and his
inability to relate to others created a serious threat to his
mental health. Gradually, he withdrew more and more
until his solitude and isolation so worried his mother
that she sought professional help.

A neurological examination suggested by the psychiatrist revealed severe visual-motor impairment, and the
EEG showed a mild convulsive pattern. Though Gary
had never had seizures, his irregular EEG pattern
prompted the doctors to prescribe anti-convulsant medication, which did in fact improve Gary's behavior and
his outlook on life. The psychological and intellectual
evaluation further indicated that Gary must be having
difficulty in school with reading and learning and recommended special attention.

Unfortunately, Gary's school had no special class for
instruction for the brain-injured. Placed instead among
the mentally retarded, the emotionally disturbed, and a
few who were just slow learners, Gary caused no more
trouble in his new class than he had previously. But
neither did he receive the individual kind of instruction

specially suited for his particular disabilities. He was left back in the second grade and continued to show no progress in his work or in making friends. His teachers were patient and kind, but although they tried to help, they simply lacked the training needed to recognize or to correct the numerous perceptual and coordination disorders involved.

After several years of individual training with an experienced ophthalmologist (including eye exercises, correction of mirror reading and reversals of certain letters) Gary had demonstrated to his mother that he could learn —but slowly. Gary's mother was now in the unenviable position of knowing more than the school authorities about her son's condition. Finally, the authorities agreed to place Gary on home instruction.[14] He was graduated from high school with a certificate[15] and sought rehabilitative vocational counseling and training at the local office of a state rehabilitation program. Eventually, he found employment in a large mail-order firm performing simple clerical tasks and intra-office messenger work.

Gary never became an extrovert or the captain of a debating team. But he did manage to become self-sufficient and responsible for his own activities. He learned how to travel by himself and to go to movies and restaurants. By participating in the program at one of several brain-injury organizations,[17] he made the acquaintance of other adolescents who had similar problems. Parents helped to organize structured recreational groups and sponsored sight-seeing trips. Initially, Gary resented having to associate with other handicapped youngsters, insisting that he had no need of his parents' restrictions and advice.

"I can take care of myself and make my own friends," he argued. "You are only holding me back."

"Is he right?" his parents pondered. "Are we over-protecting him? How can we know if and when structure becomes overprotection?"

Unfortunately, there are no hard and fast rules. Yet Gary's parents were sensitive to the right questions and they, like all parents of brain-injured children, must seek a narrow path between extremes until they arrive at the best possible adjustment for their child and his disability. Fortunately in this case, Gary realized, after several attempts to join and mingle with local teenage groups, that he could not dance, converse, or otherwise participate normally in their activities. An agonizing period of self-examination and self-rejection was followed by a healthier and more realistic acceptance of himself, his handicap, his limitations, and his strengths.

How does one evaluate Gary's story? Again we note with sadness the absence of early detection, diagnosis, or corrective treatment, and the almost inevitable development of severe maladaptive patterns of adjustment. However, after considerable fumbling and frustration, Gary did receive some help—perhaps too little, perhaps too late. Professional opinions differ about the age or critical period beyond which corrective learning may not take place.[17] Yet, how does one measure success? Certainly, not all nonhandicapped persons succeed. And just as surely, failure is not inevitable to all who are handicapped. One authority clearly states that it is not one's handicap or its severity that determines success or failure, but rather one's self-image. That Gary was able to learn beyond original expectations, that he graduated from high school, that he became independent and capable of holding a job, that he found his "identity" in the midst of adolescent turmoil—all these are testimony of success. We stand at that point in the field of brain injury where knowledge and understanding are increasing, but facilities for training specialists in the detection and treatment of the brain-injured person remain meager. The tragedy lies among the many who might have been helped. The achievements of Gary, Richie, and their parents are proof that courage and determination can help the brain-injured to experience the world as we experience it.

Parents of brain-injured children frequently benefit from professionally led discussion groups at which they share their experiences, search for better understanding, and receive help in learning how to manage their children. Many problems arise that are common to all brain-injured persons, while other characteristics may be specific to individual and family attitudes. Initially, most parents—especially mothers—feel guilty and ashamed to admit that they cannot understand or control their child's behavior. Listen to this excerpt from a group discussion among mothers.

Mrs. D. "Billy doesn't react the way my other children do. Punishing him doesn't help; reasoning with him doesn't make any difference. I must be doing something, maybe everything, wrong. It's as though he just doesn't understand what I'm talking about. He doesn't know what I mean. He wants to please, that's for sure. He is always trying to do things for me. Only he doesn't know what to do any more than I do. It's like the blind leading the blind."

Mrs. W. "That's exactly how I feel. Nothing I do or say makes an impression on Tommy. The other night I pleaded with him not to stuff himself, to behave like a gentleman and let us enjoy just one meal together without a temper tantrum.[18] I might as well have been talking to myself. First he demanded his food before everyone else. Then he picked up all his silverware and threw the fork across the table and began screaming. He ended up jumping from his chair and running around the house like—I don't know. I don't blame my husband for sending him to his room, or the other children for shouting at him to shut up. I felt like yelling and crying myself. The doctors say he's not . . . but . . . ?"

Her voice trailed off; she was too frightened to say the word or to ask the question: "Is he crazy?"

Mrs. H. "It sounds like bedtime at my house. Jimmy is driving me to distraction with his demands. 'Where's my pink towel. I want my pink towel here. Why isn't the toothpaste where it always is?' If I'm lucky and nothing is out of place, he may behave beautifully, do everything as if he were performing a ritual—wash, undress, fold his clothes. And then, suddenly, for no reason at all, he gives up, just sort of collapses.[19] He might slump to the floor and cry as if his heart were breaking. You think your son, Billy, doesn't understand you. Well, I know I don't understand Jimmy."

Having voiced their worst fears and realized that they were not alone, the mothers felt less guilt and their shame turned to relief. They even laughed about their frustrations, their very helplessness providing further release for locked-in anguish and stiffened composure. Assured that their children were not "crazy," and that their behavior could be improved, they turned their attention and energies quickly to practical matters. Furthermore, despite each mother's bewildered plea, she was closer to understanding and insight than she knew. Yes, Billy, as most brain-injured youngsters, urgently wishes to please. He wants very much to be accepted and loved.

Mrs. D. and Mrs. H. reflected two other basic facts: the child does not understand what is expected of him or how he should behave; and the adult does not understand the child's dilemma. At this point, the moderating presence of the group leader may prove especially valuable, for he may offer a few simple do's and don'ts that may guide the parents toward resolution of daily problems. He may be able to suggest the futility of trying to correct at once behavior that is a by-product of brain injury—impulsiveness, overactivity, and emotional outbursts. He should be able to indicate a far wiser course: to prepare and structure the child's environment in order to avoid and circumvent situations beyond his abilities. Here is a portion of the group leader's comment on Tommy's behavior at mealtime.

G.L. "I wonder whether pleading for gentlemanly behavior and a peaceful meal without a temper tantrum doesn't tell Tommy only that you're disappointed in him. Wouldn't it be better to serve him first? After all, he really *can't* wait. And you can cut down on his confusion by taking away his obligation to make a choice. Put only one piece of silver at his plate, and then only when it is needed.

"And you know, Mrs. H., this business of increasing the child's security by ordering his environment should work for Jimmy too. Why not, for instance, be certain that Jimmy knows exactly where to find his pink towel and his other things? Incidentally, I wouldn't encourage using the same dish or towel all the time. The trouble is that you might encourage him to perseverate and reduce his chances for carrying over the routines he has learned at home to situations he'll meet outside. A good rule of thumb is that the child's familiarity with daily routine makes him relax, and the less tense he is, the more likely he is to avoid what we call 'emotional collapse.'

"You know, we don't really have to wait for Tommy to come to the table either. It might be a good idea to rehearse the sequence of dinner—or, for that matter, any forthcoming event—beforehand. You might say, some time early in the afternoon, 'At six o'clock, Daddy will ring the bell, open the door, kiss you hello, take off his hat and coat and get washed. Then we'll all sit down for dinner. I'm going to serve you first and you can tell Daddy all about what you did today, or anything else you want to tell him. And then your brother and sister will have their chance to speak while you eat and listen. But while they're talking, you must listen and not break in.'

"Of course, when all things fail—and even the best laid plans sometimes do—just be ready for the outburst.

He may be overtired, uncertain about the order of events, or even about what is expected of him. The result —panic, explosion, or collapse. To send him to his room alone accomplishes little more than a moment's escape from a messy situation. And I completely understand that at just that moment, it's what you and the rest of the family want most. But it's also at just that moment that the child needs a mother's patient, nonpunitive, calm reassurance. Usually, all he needs is a few moments in his room with you to let the crisis pass."

The group leader went on, trying to make clear that conventional patterns of child-rearing do not work for the brain-injured. Threats of punishment, promises of reward, logical reasoning—all have absolutely no meaning for the brain-injured child since he cannot conceive of, or foresee the consequences of his actions. To be effective, a reward must be offered on the spot, with open affection and plenty of praise. Discipline, not punishment, is a must—provided that the child gains insight through simple, direct, and explicit instructions and explanations. The object of discipline is to develop insight into purposeful behavior. Since the brain-injured person has such a poor sense of the purpose of any activity, he depends upon others to explain in minute detail, with infinite patience and repetition, precisely what he must do, when and how he must do it.

By now, the parents' newfound hope again faltered.

Mrs. W. "Can they ever be cured? Will Tommy ever be accepted by others? Will it always be fights and yelling, and so little pleasure or happiness—for them or us? To help them even a little sounds like a full-time job!"

Mrs. D. "Do we have a choice? We've got to have the confidence and strength if we expect our kids to believe in themselves."

Mrs. H: "Things can't be much worse. What have I got to lose? I'm going to hire a girl to clean house and help me prepare meals for the rest of the family. I'll give Tommy his own room with a place for everything. I could make things easier for him if I could only organize my own day better. I realize now I make him wait if someone drops in, or the phone rings, and that's when he gets more excited and out of hand. From now on, everything and everyone waits while I help him over mealtime, bedtime, or a trip uptown."[20]

Results for these troubled mothers will not be discernible overnight, but their courage and persistence unquestionably pave the way for improvement for their brain-injured children and for the family structure. Perhaps the greatest value to grow out of guidance groups is the sharing of experiences in daily life and the insights into coping with everyday problems. Here is another portion of a guidance group discussion.

Mrs. F. "Richard has always been an anxious boy.[21] The least little thing used to start an emotional crisis. I feel he has really outgrown some of his early emotional outbursts. And he isn't as impulsive or irritable as he used to be either. But it didn't just happen—as all of you know. We worked pretty hard to understand Richard and tried to do everything we could at home to help him. Once we began to understand him better, through the help of his teachers and his psychiatrist, he was happier and tried hard to cooperate. It was when we all worked together that things began to fall into place.

"But I want to ask one thing. He's still pretty demanding of me and my time. I mean, I know he might get upset easily if he can't get his coat buckled or find his tie right away. I understand that. And he does have far fewer up and down moods than he used to. But other times, he'll kind of order me to do things for him. He becomes very angry and obnoxious about it too. He doesn't ask politely, or care if I have the time or energy. I've tried explaining to him that it hurts my feelings to be spoken to in that tone of voice. I've even refused to do what he asks, but that doesn't work too well either. For instance, I usually take the family's clothes to the cleaners, but Richard has a habit of demanding that I go immediately with his suit, and he can be rude. I can't make him understand that no one will want to do things for him when he speaks that way. I don't know how to help him realize the kind of impression that he makes upon others because of the way he demands things."

Mrs. L. "Can he go to the store by himself? Maybe you could turn the mess into what they call a 'success experience' for him. God knows, they need to feel capable of doing something. Why not teach him to take everyone's things to the cleaners? It would give him confidence maybe, make him feel good about helping others."

Mrs. W. "Maybe Richard is asking for proof that you won't stop helping him now that he's grown up? Do you think he might be feeling that and showing it by being bossy and demanding? I've noticed with Jerry—even though he is doing better than we ever hoped he could —there are times I think when he feels pressured and scared about whether or not he can really do what he's supposed to do. I can usually tell when he feels that way because he becomes demanding, as you say, or nasty, instead of asking for my help with his homework or whatever is bothering him. Actually, my daughter acts that way too sometimes. It's perfectly natural for anyone to get cranky when he feels insecure. But with Jerry it happens more often, is more intense, and he needs help putting things back into perspective. Let's face it—he needs me more, that's all. He's still very dependent in many ways even though he has caught up in lots of other ways."

Mrs. L. "Harold can be bossy too. He's learned to control his emotions much better. And his eating habits and table manners are 100 percent better. Remember how I used to cry and complain about that? Well, compared to then it's a pleasure to take him to a restaurant now, or to my mother's house for dinner on the holidays. What a struggle that was. First, he would just give up and feel low. Then he used to get so frustrated he would explode. It just wasn't safe to be around. Thank goodness, he can handle that now.

"But I've about given up hope for peace between him and his brother and sister. They're good kids, and they have put up with a lot on account of him in the past, but you can't blame them for getting fed up when Harold bosses them around all the time and acts as though everything is coming to him. He's so competitive, but just not as bright as they. And that has nothing to do with his disability. Still, he feels inferior. We've all put ourselves out. Oh, what a job it was years ago to get the younger ones to understand that Harold needed our help. They accused me of loving him more, paying more attention to him, and not caring about them. I think they feel that he doesn't appreciate how hard they really tried. The younger boy, Billy, has lots of friends and he goes out a lot with them, but he doesn't like to have them over to our house because Harold butts in too much and interferes with their conversations or games and insists they listen to him. He expects everyone to pay attention to him. I guess he's jealous and lonesome without friends of his own, but we do try to help him meet other brain-injured boys and girls his age. He just won't understand why his younger brother can go places and do things he can't do. And I can't keep expecting Billy to live his life according to Harold's needs."

Mrs. W. "My daughter, Terry, tried to include Jerry in her parties and outings, but she used to come home terribly upset and embarrassed. I'll never forget the evening she had a party, and, of course, Jerry assumed he was invited. A few of the boys and girls played guitar or harmonica, and Jerry announced he would sing. Well, he sang and sang and sang. It was awful. First, everyone was polite, but then Terry was ashamed of how bad he sounded and was furious with me for not stopping him. As for Jerry, he was oblivious of everyone. He has no conception of the impression he makes on others—as you said about Richard's demands and his tone of voice. Luckily, though, I remembered that Jerry had just finished memorizing a soliloquy from a play he is in at school and that saved the day. I think it has bolstered his ego too, to be in that play. He's so much more hopeful about himself and his homework now that they put him back in his regular class."

These mothers no longer yearn for easy cures. Gratefully, they acknowledge the progress that has been achieved, welcome the respite from past struggles, and realistically assess their children as individuals of varying intellectual potential. They have learned to accept the fact that the brain-injured person may not reach a level of social maturity enabling subtleties or even ease in interpersonal relations. And they know too that he may always find it difficult to empathize with others on any but an emotionally shallow level. But they also know that he can learn basic social skills and that he must be helped to develop better social judgment.

As we have seen, the future of these children is not bleak. Parents and professionals continue to confront the challenge. Their efforts justify the optimism of leaders in the field. That optimism is rooted in the faith that unified efforts by responsible adults and professionals—if combined with specialized educational curricula adjusted to individual needs—can arrest the malfunction of the brain-injured child, can change the direction of his maladaptive patterns of response, and can rehabilitate him.

POSTSCRIPT

Recent Research in Educational Methods for the Brain-Injured: A Survey in Brief

Even after accord is reached about the definition of brain injury, its cause, prevention, etiology, dynamics, and prognosis, the crucial query remains: How can we best help the brain-injured individual to live more compatibly in the only world available to him? The answer may fall most plainly within the province of education. While controversy continues about the most suitable method of teaching, it has been demonstrated that most brain-injured youngsters can learn—*if* they are given the proper environment, personnel, and techniques specifically adapted to their particular deficiencies. Furthermore, there is fundamental agreement about basic educational principles pertinent to the brain-injured. Different educational strategies may regroup major brain-injured characteristics, stress one factor over another, use variant terminology, or suggest alternate corrective procedures. Nevertheless, all of these characteristics have been subsumed in every method of instruction thus far put forth.

Most authorities agree that the time-honored educational concept stressing "individual differences" finds renewed meaning and vigor when applied to education of the brain-injured. Despite the highly individualized patterns among the diverse symptoms of brain injury, common traits do exist. Thus, a number of educational methods have been devised in the past twenty years to serve a host of brain-injured youngsters fortunate enough to receive such instruction. Few professionals disagree about the following basic elements in any educational program:

Early corrective measures are indispensable.

Conventional teaching methods are inadequate.

New, not remedial, materials and methods are required.

Special techniques for specific impairments are essential.

Highly skilled teachers are critically needed.

Prolonged neglect and isolation from regular classrooms can be damaging.

Unimpaired strengths must be developed while deviations are being corrected.

The earliest and most comprehensive of these educational programs was developed by Alfred Strauss and Laura Lehtinen (1947; see also Strauss and Kephart 1955; Strauss and Werner 1942) and elaborated upon more recently by William Cruickshank and G. Orville Johnson (1967) in *Education of Exceptional Children and Youth.* Cruickshank adheres to the learning theory based on successful conditioning which in turn, he feels, leads to logical understanding, improved self-concepts and body-image, and a healthier integrated ego. Five major aspects of his educational program for brain-injured children center on the pivotal use of structure.

1. Because the brain-injured child has difficulty relating to others, the relationship structure is crucial for realistic and positive learning. The teacher must fully understand each child—his total pathology, his level of tolerance for frustration, his attention span, his native intellectual potential, as well as his unique personal lifestyle. And he must maintain the relationship despite abuse, distrust, and failure. The child needs to be accepted on his own terms. He should learn to behave within clearly defined limits and should be responded to in a consistent fashion. (Cruickshank 1967a and 1967b).

2. No less important in the total educational program is the need to structure an environment in order to compensate for the brain-injured child's chief characteristic —his inability to cope with stimuli. To this purpose, all stimuli—particularly visual and auditory—must be minimized. Small rooms with individual cubicles and fixed desks are recommended, with few or no large open spaces (auditoriums, cafeterias, gymnasiums).

3. Structuring the daily program and ordering the life space for the child with brain injury enhances his chance to succeed, make predictions, improve his self-image and strengthen his ego. He becomes more secure when he knows where and when to rest, to have lunch, how to ask for assistance, how to return items to their proper place, and how to dress himself.

4. The greatest challenge for creative teaching lies in the realm of structuring the materials to achieve the fullest correction of faulty skills. The child's unimpaired abilities need to be developed while the teacher is simultaneously teaching to the disability. Concise educational and psychological evaluations that elaborate upon the child's attention span, dissociative and perseverative tendencies, figure-ground reversals, controls, space orientation, and body-image assist the teacher (and her assistant) in selecting equipment suitable to each child and his particular deficiency. Specific techniques and devices have been developed to help the brain-injured child correct and overcome underlying perceptual and conceptual disturbances and behavioral disorders that have seriously impeded his ability to learn how to read, understand numbers, draw or write, or develop normal speech and language skills. (Bortner 1968:131–46; Cruickshank 1967b: 276–79; see also chapters

by Freidus, Hardy, Gardner, and Kephart in Cruick-shank 1966).

5. To acquire a healthy body-image at least thirty minutes a day should be devoted to motor training. The child needs to develop an awareness of the relationship between the parts of his body and the whole and of his relationship in space. Likewise, better coordination of legs and arms are basic to learning how to write.

Finally, Cruickshank reminds potential educators not to neglect the daily instruction in speech and language that will accelerate the developmental lag in communication and language skills (Eisonson 1956; Frostig 1966).

A vast body of material has become available as professional workers in various disciplines continue to add to our knowledge. In this account, only brief reference can be made to their notable contributions. Marianne Frostig's work in testing and training in visual-perceptual materials is familiar to all in the field (Frostig 1968; Frostig and Horne 1964; Frostig, LeFever, and Whittlesey 1964; Gallagher 1966). The Marianne Frostig Developmental Test of Visual Perception, the Illinois Test of Psycholinguistic Abilities developed by Samuel Kirk[22] and the Wepman Test of Auditory Discrimination (Wepman 1958) are well-known tests used in comprehensive educational evaluation of the brain-injured.

Gerald Getman (Getman 1964; Getman and Hendrickson 1966) has investigated the development of visuo-motor skills and their relationship to academic performance of the brain-injured. Regretting the need to have still to distinguish, even for professionals, between an *eye* and/or *vision* problem, he dutifully reminds us that vision is more than acuity. Acuity or clearness of sight is tested by the usual eye tests, whereas vision is learned and has to do with perceptual, integrative functions. Beginning with the need for adequate *eye-movement, eye teaming* skills, and *eye-hand* coordination skills, he stresses the importance of eye movement for optimum vision. Further along, he discusses the development of good visual form and refractive problems, both as outgrowths of the more basic underlying processes of visual performance.

H. Myklebust, Miriam Hardy, et al. (Myklebust 1957) remind us that there is a similar need for emphasis on the auditory integrating system since the role of auditory perception is vital to the learning process. Difficulty in auditory discrimination, auditory-sequential learning or the inability to associate auditory patterns with visual patterns can successfully sabotage any learning process.

N. Kephart, C. Newell, *et al.* (Kephart 1968, 1960, 1966) have made significant progress in the areas of diagnosis and training of perceptual-motor skills. The development of motor patterns—locomotion (as distinguished from motor skills like walking or jumping)—permits environmental exploration for the purpose of accumulating information. Next, the child must learn *motor generalization* as an aid to the development of adequate space-time structure. He must learn, in other words, how to maintain balance in relation to gravity, how to observe the relationship of objects in space, how to contact by reaching, grasping, and releasing—and finally, the generalization of *receipt* and *propulsion*, i.e. the investigation of movement toward himself and away from himself. Once the child inhabits a motor world in which he moves and responds, he needs to perfect the "perceptual-motor match process." Let us assume, for example, that the child now possesses a body of information he has learned from his motor exploration into his environment. He must continuously integrate new incoming perceptual (auditory, visual, tactile, etc.) information with previous motor information or be doomed to respond in an inappropriate or bizarre manner. To accomplish these goals, Kephart suggests that teachers of the brain-injured child be developmentally oriented. Moreover, although all learning should be directed to the development of generalizations, it is of the utmost importance to determine a child's present structure fully and to identify his strongest areas of performance while strengthening his weaker abilities.

It is generally acknowledged that such problems of integration or generalization for the brain-injured child occur on all developmental levels—perceptual, motor and learning. Embracing all three, Riley M. Gardner (1966) has nonetheless directed his investigations particularly toward the latter aspect of the effects of brain damage—the development of *cognitive structures*. Among the elements Gardner has explored of faulty cognitive performance by the brain-injured, and of its relationship to the learning process are these: the severe limitations of being unable to sustain thoughts consciously (momentary span of attention); the inability to discriminate between the essential and nonessential (impairment of selectivity); the fluctuating level of attending to a task (attentional intensity); faulty scanning skills; inadequate concept formation and ineffective memory formation.

Brain-injury presents the greatest challenge to the profession of rehabilitation. The symptoms are recognizable, though the defect itself and its causes are not readily exhibited. Although we do not fully understand the brain-injured person, we now know that he can be helped. Sadly, much more is understood than is being put into practice. More refined diagnostic tools exist, better methods and techniques of treatment and education have been developed. However, there is far too much lag in the training of qualified people needed to work with the brain-injured as part of a cohesive, interdisciplinary unit. Until we perceive the problem of the brain-injured person as a whole, we can only linger in chaos and delay the help these people so urgently need if they are to share in whatever joys a more orderly world may afford them.

NOTES

1. Chronic brain syndrome; brain-injured children (minimal); minimal neurological handicap; minimal cerebral dysfunction; perceptual handicap; cognitive defect; maturational lag; child with language disorders; hyperactive child; neuro-physiological immaturity; learning disability; CNS (central nervous system) disorder; minimal brain dysfunction; neurologically handicapped child; brain-damaged; hyperkinetic child, and so on.

2. "Dr. DiCarlo says that 20% of all children in M.R. classes are undiagnosed and untreated brain-injured children" (Kastein 1962).

3. *Cerebral palsy* is a brain disorder resulting from injury to gross motor centers with impaired muscle control and sensation.

Epilepsy is an organic disorder of the brain having to do with injured brain cells.

Mental retardation is limited intelligence due to severe brain damage or faulty developmental processes.

4. Cruickshank explains his choice of the term *brain-injured* instead of minimal brain dysfunction: "There is nothing minimal about the

impact of tissue injury of whatsoever nature or extent on the child or on his attempts to deal with it from the point of view of learning, ego development, and total personality integrity" (Cruickshank 1966). Another authority considers these difficulties to be *maturational lags* of specific developmental processes and urges that these not be confused with irreparable structural defects (Bender 1956).

5. Vision and hearing may be adequate, but there may be serious visual or auditory perceptual problems.

6. Wechsler Adult Intelligence Scale, Wechsler Intelligence Scale for Children, Stanford Binet Intelligence Scale, Bender-Gestalt Visual Motor Test, Frostig Developmental Test of Visual Perception, Illinois Test of Psycholinguistic Abilities (ITPA), Story Recall, Sorting Test, Wepman Test of Auditory Discrimination, Rorschach, and others.

7. Some authorities explain perseveration as serving a tension-release device through motor activity. Others suggest a compensatory or self-protective value through perseveration. (Kastein and Klapper 1962: 86).

8. His difficulty relating cause and effect partially explains the frustration parents and teachers experience in their search for effective discipline.

9. Although body-image disturbances may be associated with a variety of illnesses (toxic or metabolic disorders; amputations; or psychological problems), we are primarily concerned here with body-image disturbance as a consequence of neurological impairment of the sensory or motor systems and as a function of adolescence. For a history of the development of the body-image concept and its disturbances derived from neurological and psychoanalytic practices, see Kolb 1959.

10. Sarason readily acknowledges that brain injury affects behavior, but he cautions against automatically attributing all pathological behavior to the same brain damage (Sarason 1964).

11. The American Psychiatric Association lists five symptoms of Organic Brain Syndrome: impairment of orientation; impairment of memory; impairment of all intellectual functions such as comprehension, calculation, knowledge, learning, etc.; impairment of judgment; and lability and shallowness of affect (*The Diagnostic and Statistical Manual of Mental Disorders* 1968: 22).

12. Michal-Smith and Murry Morgenstern describe the brain-injured child who is adjusted to his environment with adequate per-

formance and satisfaction, freedom from tension and anxiety. He is a somewhat rigid, passive, contented individual who relates to simple, immediate tasks and can meet his restricted needs without too much outer conflict or inner disorganization (Michal-Smith and Morgenstern 1962: 63).

13. It has been suggested by some authorities that efforts to develop compulsive behavior might benefit those brain-injured persons who are excessively fragmented or disorganized in thought and action.

14. Home instruction refers to the educational practice of sending a teacher into the home for children who are severely disabled—physically or emotionally—and who cannot attend school. Other kinds of educational provisions may be found in hospital schools, institutions, sheltered-care facilities, special schools or classes, and itinerant or remedial teacher programs.

15. Some progressive schools have adopted the practice of graduating handicapped students (despite a lower level of academic achievement) with a certificate in place of a diploma.

16. The Association for Children with Learning Disabilities (ACLD), the National Society for Crippled Children and Adults, the Neurological and Sensory Disease Service Program, and the New York Association for Brain Injured Children.

17. Factors other than age are often crucial. A child with superior intelligence, though brain-injured, may do honors work in high school and college—providing, of course, he receive corrective education. Lauretta Bender and others vigorously oppose isolation of the brain-injured child for extensive periods of time, arguing that this may cause irreparable damage to his future rehabilitation. To date, however, too little has been done for the majority of brain-injured teenagers to allow for a definitive conclusion as to whether there is a point beyond which they cannot learn.

18. Sometimes a child's inability to stop eating has been explained as perseverated activity.

19. This kind of behavior is sometimes referred to as an emotional collapse or, as Goldstein has called it, a catastrophic reaction (see Goldstein 1959). For another view, see Lewis, Strauss, and Lehtinen 1960: 74.

20. Michal-Smith describes the ideal parents for a brain-injured child to find optimal adjustment. The mother should be a comfortable, orderly person, and the father an accountant type who does not

become upset too easily. Neither should be hysterical or disorganized (Michal-Smith 1962).

21. Phyllis Greenacre (1941) has written about the brain-injured person's "predisposition to anxiety" as a generic trait.

22. This test provides a quantitative measure in nine different psycholinguistic abilities, greatly improving evaluation of areas of weakness and strength: 1. Auditory Decoding Test, for understanding of spoken language;   2. Visual Decoding Test, to determine how well a child understands the significance of pictured items;   3. Auditory-Vocal Association, to see if he can associate elements of spoken language and respond vocally and correctly;   4. Visual-Motor Association Test, for association of objects or pictures which belong together (no aural or oral);   5. Vocal Encoding Test, for vocal expressions about objects seen and held;   6. Motor Encoding Test, for expression by gestures, without vocal response;   7. Auditory Vocal Automatic Test concerning elementary grammatical constructions of language;   8. Auditory Vocal Sequential Test, for auditory memory for digits;   9. Visual Motor Sequential Test, for assessment of sequential visual-memory (Kirk 1962: 268).

REFERENCES

Arieti, S., ed., *American Handbook of Psychiatry*, 3 vols., New York, Basic Books, 1959.

Bender, Lauretta, "The Brain-Damaged Child," in *Special Education for the Exceptional*, Merle Frampton and Elena Gall, eds., 3 vols., Boston, Porter Sargent, 1956: 3 48–61.

Bortner, Morton, ed., *Evaluation and Education of Children with Brain Damage*, Springfield, Ill., Charles C Thomas, 1968.

Cruickshank, William M., "Current Educational Practices with Exceptional Children," in *Education of Exceptional Children and Youth*, 2d ed., William M. Cruickshank and G. Orville Johnson, eds., Englewood Cliffs, N.J., Prentice-Hall, 1967: 45–98. [Cruickshank 1967a]

Cruickshank, William M., "The Education of the Child with Brain Injury," in *Education of Exceptional Children and Youth*, 2d ed., William M. Cruickshank and G. Orville Johnson, eds., Englewood Cliffs, N.J., Prentice-Hall, 1967: 238–83. [Cruickshank 1967b.]

Cruickshank, William M., ed., *The Teacher of Brain-Injured Children*, Syracuse, N.Y., Syracuse University Press, 1966.

Cruickshank, William M., and G. Orville Johnson, eds., *Education of Exceptional Children and Youth*, 2d ed., Englewood Cliffs, N.J., Prentice-Hall, 1967.

Diagnostic and Statistical Manual of Mental Disorders, The, Washington, D.C., American Psychiatric Association, 1968.

Eisonson, J., "Aphasia in Brain-Injured Children," in *Special Education for the Exceptional*, Merle Frampton and Elena Gall, eds., 3 vols., Boston, Porter Sargent, 1956: *3*, 73–76.

Frostig, Marianne, "The Needs of Teachers for Specialized Information on Reading," in *The Teacher of Brain-Injured Children*, William M. Cruickshank, ed., Syracuse, N.Y., Syracuse University Press, 1966: 87–109.

Frostig, Marianne, "A Treatment Program for Children with Learning Difficulties," in *Evaluation and Education of Children with Brain Damage*, Morton Bortner, ed., Springfield, Ill., Charles C Thomas, 1968: 223–42.

Frostig, Marianne, and David Horne, *The Frostig Program for the Development of Visual Perception*, Chicago, Follett, 1964.

Frostig, Marianne, D. W. LeFever, and J. R. B. Whittlesey, *The Marianne Frostig Developmental Test of Visual Perception*, 3d ed., Palo Alto, Calif., Consulting Psychologists Press, 1964.

Gallagher, James J., "Children with Developmental Imbalances: A Psycho-Educational Definition," in *The Teacher of Brain-Injured Children*, William M. Cruickshank, ed., Syracuse, N.Y., Syracuse University Press, 1966: 21–43.

Gardner, Riley M., "The Needs of Teachers for Specialized Information on the Development of Cognitive Structures," in *The Teacher of Brain-Injured Children*, William M. Cruickshank, ed., Syracuse, N.Y., Syracuse University Press, 1966: 137–52.

Getman, Gerald N., "The Primary Visual Abilities Essential to Academic Achievement," in *Child Vision Care*, Duncan, Okla., Optometric Extension Program, 1964.

Getman, Gerald N., and Homer H. Hendrickson, "The Needs of Teachers for Specialized Information on the Development of Visuomotor Skills in Relation to Academic Performance," in *The Teacher of Brain-Injured Children*, William M. Cruickshank, ed., Syracuse, N.Y., Syracuse University Press, 1966: 153–168.

Goldstein, Kurt, "Functional Disturbances in Brain Damage," in

American Handbook of Psychiatry, S. Arieti, ed., 3 vols., New York, Basic Books, 1959: Vol. I, 770–94.

Greenacre, Phyllis, "Predisposition to Anxiety," *Psychoanalytic Quarterly 10* (1941): 66–94; 610–38.

Kastein, Shulamith, "Speech and Language Habilitation in a Post-Encephalitic Child," in *The Special Child: Diagnosis, Treatment, and Habilitation*, H. Michal-Smith and Shulamith Kastein, eds., Seattle, Special Child Publications, 1962: 65–77.

Kastein, Shulamith, and Zelda S. Klapper, "Integrative Therapy for the Brain-Injured Child: A Case Study," in *The Special Child: Diagnosis, Treatment, and Habilitation*, H. Michal-Smith and Shulamith Kastein, eds., Seattle, Special Child Publication, 1962: 79–90.

Kephart, Newell C., "The Needs of Teachers for Specialized Information on Perception," in *The Teacher of Brain-Injured Children*, William M. Cruickshank, ed., Syracuse, N.Y., Syracuse University Press, 1966: 169–80.

Kephart, Newell C., *The Slow Learner in the Classroom*, Columbus, Ohio, C. E. Merrill, 1960.

Kephart, Newell C., "Teaching the Child with a Perceptual-Motor Handicap," in *Evaluation and Education of Children with Brain Damage*, Morton Bortner, ed., Springfield, Ill., Charles C Thomas, 1968: 147–92.

Kirk, Samuel A., *Educating Exceptional Children*, Boston, Houghton Mifflin, 1962.

Kolb, Lawrence C., "Disturbances of the Body-Image," in *American Handbook of Psychiatry*, S. Arieti, ed., 3 vols., New York, Basic Books, 1959: Vol. I, 749–69.

Lewis, Richard S., Alfred A. Strauss, and Laura E. Lehtinen, *The Other Child*, New York, Grune and Stratton, 1960.

Michal-Smith, H., "Adjustment of the Neurologically Impaired," in *The Special Child: Diagnosis, Treatment, and Habilitation*," H. Michal-Smith and Shulamith Kastein, eds., Seattle, Special Child Publications, 1962: 91–106.

Michal-Smith, H., and Shulamith Kastein, eds., *The Special Child: Diagnosis, Treatment, and Habilitation*, Seattle, Special Child Publications, 1962.

Michal-Smith, H., and Murry Morgenstern, "Psycho-dynamics of the Brain-Injured Child," in *The Special Child: Diagnosis, Treatment, and Habilitation*, H. Michal-Smith and Shulamith Kastein, eds., Seattle, Special Child Publications, 1962: 45–64.

Myklebust, Helmer R., "Aphasia in Children—Language Pathology and Diagnosis and Training," in *Handbook of Speech Pathology*, Lee Edward Travis, ed., New York, Appleton-Century-Crofts, 1957: 516–25.

Rappaport, Sheldon R., "Behavior and Ego Development in a Brain-Injured Child," *Psychoanalytic Study of the Child 16* (1961): 423–50.

Sarason, Seymour B., "Some Aspects of the Brain-Behavior Problem," in *The Special Child in Century 21*, Jerome Hellmuth, ed., Seattle, Special Child Publications, 1964: 47–55.

Strauss, Alfred A., and Newell C. Kephart, *Psychopathology and Education of the Brain-Injured Child, Vol. 2*, New York, Grune & Stratton, 1955.

Strauss, Alfred A., and Laura E. Lehtinen, *Psychopathology and Education of the Brain-Injured Child, Vol. 1*, New York, Grune & Stratton, 1947.

Strauss, Alfred A., and H. Werner, "Disorders of Conceptual Thinking in the Brain Injured Child," *Journal of Nervous Mental Disease 96* (1942): 153–72.

Wepman, J. M., *Wepman Test of Auditory Discrimination*, Chicago, Language Research Associates, 1958.

Bibliography

ABRAMSON, HAROLD A., *Psychological Problems in the Father-Son Relationship: A Case of Eczema and Asthma*, New York, October House, 1969.

AGLE, DAVID P., and A. Mattson, *Emotional Health in Hemophilia*, New York, National Hemophilia Foundation, n.d.

ALLEN, FREDERICK M., "Diabetes Mellitus," in *Encyclopedia Americana 9*, New York, Americana Corp. (1967): 54.

Arieti, S., ed., *American Handbook of Psychiatry*, 3 vols., New York, Basic Books, 1959.

Barrows, Howard S., and Eli S. Goldensohn, *Handbook for Parents*, New York, Ayerst Laboratories, n.d.

Bender, Lauretta, "The Brain-Damaged Child," in *Special Education for the Exceptional*, Merle Frampton and Elena Gall, eds., 3 vols. Boston, Porter Sargent, 1956: *3*, 48–61.

Bortner, Morton, ed., *Evaluation and Education of Children with Brain Damage*, Springfield, Ill., Charles C Thomas, 1968.

Bruch, Hilde, "Physiologic and Psychologic Interrelationships in Diabetes in Children," *Psychosomatic Medicine* 11 (1949): 200–210.

Cruickshank, William M., "Current Educational Practices with Exceptional Children," in *Education of Exceptional Children and Youth*, 2d ed., William M. Cruickshank and G. Orville Johnson, eds., Englewood Cliffs, N.J., Prentice-Hall, 1967: 45–98.

Cruickshank, William M., "The Education of the Child with Brain Injury," in *Education of Exceptional Children and Youth*, 2d ed., William M. Cruickshank and G. Orville Johnson, eds., Englewood Cliffs, N.J., Prentice-Hall, 1967: 238–83.

Cruickshank, William M., ed., *The Teacher of Brain-Injured Children*, Syracuse, N.Y., Syracuse University Press, 1966.

Cruickshank, William M., and G. Orville Johnson, eds., *Education of Exceptional Children and Youth*, 2d ed., Englewood Cliffs, N.J., Prentice-Hall, 1967.

"Detecting an Old Killer," *Time* (Oct. 4, 1971): 57.

Deutsch, Patricia, and Ron Deutsch, "One Man's Fight Against Hemophilia," *Today's Health* 45 (1967): 40–43.

The Diagnostic and Statistical Manual of Mental Disorders, Washington, D.C., American Psychiatric Association, 1968.

Didisheim, Paul, "Mechanism of Bleeding and Hemostasis in the Hemophilias," *Hemophilia vol. 1, no. 1*, 1966.

Diggs, L. W., "Sickle Cell Disease," *Journal of the American Medical Association* 218 (1971): 1054.

"Discriminating Disease," *Time* (Dec. 21, 1970): 41.

Dolger, Henry, and Bernard Seeman, *How to Live with Diabetes*, New York, W. W. Norton, 1965.

Eisonson, J., "Aphasia in Brain-Injured Children," in *Special*

Education for the Exceptional, Merle Frampton and Elena Gall, eds., 3 vols., Boston, Porter Sargent, 1956: *3*.

Epilepsy: The Facts, Washington, D.C., Epilepsy Foundation of America, 1967.

Epilepsy: A Survey of State Laws, Washington, D.C., Epilepsy Foundation of America, 1968.

Facts About Diabetes, New York, American Diabetes Association, 1966.

Feinberg, Samuel M., *Living with Your Allergy*, Philadelphia, J. B. Lippincott, 1968.

Feingold, Ben F., Margaret Thaler Singer, Edith H. Freeman, and Andrew Deskins, "Psychological Variables in Allergic Disease: A Critical Appraisal of Methodology," *Journal of Allergy 37* (Sep. 1966): 152–53.

Fink, Geraldine, and Henry I. Schneer, "Psychiatric Evaluation of Adolescent Asthmatics," in *The Asthmatic Child*, Henry I. Schneer, ed., New York, Harper and Row, 1963: 205–24.

Frampton, Merle, and Elena Gall, eds., *Special Education for the Exceptional*, 3 vols., Boston, Porter Sargent, 1956.

French, T. M., et al., "Psychogenic Factors in Bronchial Asthma," *Psychosomatic Medicine Monographs*, Parts I and II, Washington, D.C., National Research Council, 1941.

Frostig, Marianne, "The Needs of Teachers for Specialized Information on Reading," in *The Teacher of Brain-Injured Children*, William M. Cruickshank, ed., Syracuse, N.Y., Syracuse University Press, 1966: 87–109.

Frostig, Marianne, "A Treatment Program for Children with Learning Difficulties," in *Evaluation and Education of Children with Brain Damage*, Morton Bortner, ed., Springfield, Ill., Charles C Thomas, 1968: 223–42.

Frostig, Marianne, and David Horne, *The Frostig Program for the Development of Visual Perception*, Chicago, Follett, 1964.

Frostig, Marianne, D. W. LeFever, and J. R. B. Whittlesey, *The Marianne Frostig Developmental Test of Visual Perception*, 3d ed., Palo Alto, Calif., Consulting Psychologists Press, 1964.

Gallagher, James J., "Children with Developmental Imbalances: A Psycho-Educational Definition," in *The Teacher of Brain-Injured Children*, William M. Cruickshank, ed., Syracuse, N.Y., Syracuse University Press, 1966: 21–43.

Gardner, Riley M., "The Needs of Teachers for Specialized Information on the Development of Cognitive Structures," in *The Teacher of Brain-Injured Children*, William M. Cruickshank, ed., Syracuse, N.Y., Syracuse University Press, 1966: 137–52.

Getman, Gerald N., "The Primary Visual Abilities Essential to Academic Achievement," in *Child Vision Care*, Duncan, Okla., Optometric Extension Program, 1964.

Getman, Gerald N., and Homer H. Hendrickson, "The Needs of Teachers for Specialized Information on the Development of Visuomotor Skills in Relation to Academic Performance," in *The Teacher of Brain-Injured Children*, William M. Cruickshank, ed., Syracuse, N.Y., Syracuse University Press, 1966: 153–68.

Goldensohn, Eli S., and Howard S. Barrows, *Handbook for Patients*, New York, Ayerst Laboratories, n.d.

Goldstein, Kurt, "Functional Disturbances in Brain Damage," in *American Handbook of Psychiatry*, S. Arieti, ed., 3 vols., New York, Basic Books, 1959: *1*, 770–94.

Greenacre, Phyllis, "Predisposition to Anxiety, *Psychoanalytic Quarterly 10* (1941): 66–94, 610–38.

Handbook for the Asthmatic, New York, Allergy Foundation of America, 1966.

Harris, M. Coleman, and Norman Shure, *All About Allergy*, Englewood Cliffs, N.J., Prentice-Hall, 1969.

Hay Fever... and What You Can Do About It, rev. ed., New York, Allergy Foundation of America, 1966.

"Help for Hemophiliacs," *Time*, August 16, 1968.

Hemophiliac and His School, The, New York, National Hemophilia Foundation, n.d.

Kastein, Shulamith, "Speech and Language Habilitation in a Post-Encephalitic Child," in *The Special Child: Diagnosis, Treatment, and Habilitation*, H. Michal-Smith and Shulamith Kastein, eds., Seattle, Special Child Publications, 1962: 65–77.

Kastein, Shulamith, and Zelda S. Klapper, "Integrative Therapy for the Brain-Injured Child: A Case Study," in *The Special Child: Diagnosis, Treatment, and Habilitation*, H. Michal-Smith and Shulamith Kastein, eds., Seattle, Special Child Publication, 1962: 79–90.

Katz, Alfred H., "Social Adaptation in Chronic Illness: A Study of Hemophilia," *American Journal of Public Health and the Nation's Health 53* (1963): 1660–75.

Kennedy, W. B., "Psychologic Problems of the Young Diabetic," *Diabetes 4* (1955): 207–209.

Kephart, Newell C., "The Needs of Teachers for Specialized Information on Perception," in *The Teacher of Brain-Injured Children*, William M. Cruickshank, ed., Syracuse, N.Y., Syracuse University Press, 1966: 169–80.

Kephart, Newell C., *The Slow Learner in the Classroom*, Columbus, Ohio, C. E. Merrill, 1960.

Kephart, Newell C., "Teaching the Child with a Perceptual-Motor Handicap," in *Evaluation and Education of Children with Brain Damage*, Morton Bortner, ed., Springfield, Ill., Charles C Thomas, 1968: 147–92.

Kessler, Henry R., *Rehabilitation of the Physically Handicapped*, rev. ed., New York, Columbia University Press, 1958.

Kirk, Samuel A., *Educating Exceptional Children*, Boston, Houghton Mifflin, 1962.

Kleeman, Susan T., "Psychiatric Contributions in the Treatment of Asthma," *Annals of Allergy* 25 (1967): 611–19.

Kolb, Lawrence C., "Disturbances of the Body-Image," in *American Handbook of Psychiatry*, S. Arieti, ed., 3 vols., New York, Basic Books 1959: 1, 749–69.

Kram, Charles, "Epilepsy in Children and Youth" in *Psychology of Exceptional Children and Youth*, 2d ed., William M. Cruickshank, ed., Englewood Cliffs, N.J., Prentice-Hall, 1963: 369–393.

Lewis, Jessica H., "The Inheritance of Hemophilia," *Hemophilia vol. 1, no. 1*, 1966.

Lewis, Richard S., Alfred A. Strauss, and Laura E. Lehtinen, *The Other Child*, New York, Grune and Stratton, 1960.

McGovern, John P., and James A. Knight, *Allergy and Human Emotion*, Springfield, Ill., Charles C Thomas, 1957.

Michal-Smith, H., "Adjustment of the Neurologically Impaired," in *The Special Child: Diagnosis, Treatment, and Habilitation*, H. Michal-Smith and Shulamith Kastein, eds., Seattle, Special Child Publications, 1962: 91–106.

Michal-Smith, H., and Shulamith Kastein, eds., *The Special Child: Diagnosis, Treatment, and Habilitation*, Seattle, Special Child Publications, 1962.

Michal-Smith, H., and Murry Morgenstern, "Psycho-dynamics of the Brain-Injured Child," in *The Special Child: Diagnosis, Treatment, and Habilitation*, H. Michal-Smith and Shulamith Kastein, eds., Seattle, Special Child Publications, 1962: 45–64.

Myklebust, Helmer R., "Aphasia in Children—Language Pathology and Diagnosis and Training," in *Handbook of Speech Pathology*, Lee Edward Travis, ed., New York, Appleton-Century-Crofts, 1957: 516–25.

Nalbandian, Robert M., "Sickle-Cell Crisis: A New Approach to Treatment," *Drug Therapy* (Feb. 1971): 56–57.

Nalbandian, Robert M., et al., "Sickledex Test for Hemoglobin S.: A Critique," *Journal of the American Medical Association 218* (1971): 1679–82.

"New Strategy for Sickle Cell Disease," *Journal of the American Medical Association 218* (1971): 1693–94.

New York Times, Sept. 8, 1968, Section IV, p. 7, col 1.

Newman, Joseph, "Psychological Problems of Children and Youth with Chronic Medical Disorders," in *Psychology of Exceptional Children and Youth*, 2d ed., William M. Cruickshank, ed., Englewood Cliffs, N.J., Prentice-Hall, 1963: 394–447.

"Now Eddie Smith Has a Better Chance of Getting His Rhodes Scholarship," *Today's Health* (Dec. 1971): 55–56.

Patient's Guide to Electroencephalography, A, Washington, D.C., Epilepsy Foundation of America, n.d.

Rappaport, Sheldon R., "Behavior and Ego Development in a Brain-Injured Child," *Psychoanalytic Study of the Child 16* (1961): 423–50.

Rubin, Benjamin, and Paul Levine, *Care and Treatment of Teeth of Hemophiliacs*, New York, National Hemophilia Foundation, 1966.

Rubin, Benjamin, Paul Levine, and Martin C. Rosenthal, "Complete Dental Care of the Hemophiliac," *Oral Surgery, Oral Medicine, and Oral Pathology 12, no. 6* (1959): 665–75.

Sands, Harry, and Jacqueline Seaver, *Epilepsy—Today's Encouraging Outlook*, New York, Public Affairs Committee, 1966.

Sarason, Seymour B., "Some Aspects of the Brain-Behavior Problem," in *The Special Child in Century 21*, Jerome Hellmuth, ed., Seattle, Special Child Publications, 1964: 47–55.

Scott, Robert B., "Health Care Priority and Sickle Cell Anemia," *Journal of the American Medical Association 214* (1970): 731–34.

Scott, Robert B., "Sickle-Cell Anemia—High Prevalence and Low Priority," *New England Journal of Medicine 282* (Jan. 14, 1970): 164–65.

Sickle Cell Anemia—A Tragic Burden for Millions of Americans, New York, Foundation for Research and Education in Sickle Cell Disease, n.d.

Skin and Its Allergies, The, New York, Allergy Foundation of America, 1966.

Strauss, Alfred A., and Newell C. Kephart, *Psychopathology and Education of the Brain-Injured Child, Vol. 2*, New York, Grune and Stratton, 1955.

Strauss, Alfred A., and Laura E. Lehtinen, *Psychopathology and Education of the Brain-Injured Child, Vol. 1*, New York, Grune and Stratton, 1947.

Strauss, Alfred A., and H. Werner, "Disorders of Conceptual Thinking in the Brain-Injured Child," *Journal of Nervous Mental Disease 96* (1942): 153–72.

Strauss, Herbert S., *Diagnosis and Treatment of Hemophilia*, Boston, Children's Hospital Medical Center, 1967.

Teacher Tips, Washington, D.C., Epilepsy Foundation of America, n.d.

U.S. Civil Service Commission, *Employment of Diabetics in the Federal Service*, Washington, D.C., Government Printing Office, 1956.

U.S. Department of Health, Education, and Welfare, Public Health Service, "Sickle Cell Anemia—What Is It?" *Public Health Service Publication No. 1341, Health Information Series No. 119*, Washington, D.C., Government Printing Office, n.d.

U.S. Department of Health, Education, and Welfare, Social and Rehabilitation Service, Rehabilitation Services Administration, *A Survey of Medicine and Medical Practice for the Rehabilitation Counselor*, Washington, D.C., Government Printing Office, 1966.

Uslick, John F., D.O., "Sickle Cell Disease Associated with Beta Thalassemia: Report of a Case," *Journal of the American Osteopathic Association 69* (1970): 583–600.

Wepman, J. M., *Wepman Test of Auditory Discrimination*, Chicago, Language Research Associates, 1958.

World Journal Tribune, New York, April 23, 1967, B5.

Index

AHF factor, and hemophilia, 44, 57, 58 n.2
AHG factor, and hemophila, 58 n.2
Allergic rhinitis, 121
  cause, 121
  symptoms, 121
Allergies, 104–31 *See also* Bronchial asthma, Contact dermatitis, Eczema, Hay Fever, Hives
  age groupings, 105
  allergens, 104, 107
  antigens, 104, 107
  antigen-antibody reaction, 107, 122
  causes, 105, 106
  complications, 105, 110, 122
  definition of, 104
  diagnosis, 105, 108
    allergy skin tests, 108–9
    bronchial inhalation test, 109
    conjunctival test, 109
    nasal inhalation test, 109
    nasal instillation test, 109
    passive-transfer test, 108–9
    patch test, 109
    scratch test, 108
  in history, 106–7
  shock organ, 105, 110, 122
  Skin allergies, 109–17
  symptoms, 106
  treatment, 105
    drugs, 105
    desensitization, 105
American Academy of Allergy, Pollen Survey Committee, 120
American Diabetic Association, 86–87
Antihemophilic factor, 58 n.2
Association for Children with Learning Disabilities (ACLD), 171 n.16

Banting, Frederick, 74–75
Bender, Lauretta, 171 n.17
Bender-Gestalt Visual Motor Test, 170 n.6
Best Charles, 74–75
Blackley, Charles, 107
Bleeding time, in hemophilia, 43, 58 n.4
Blodgett Memorial Hospital, 66
Bostock, John, 107
Brain injury (minimal brain-dys-

DATE DUE			
OCT 18 '79	OCT 19 '79		
APR 29 '80	APR 23 '80		
OCT 27 '80	OCT 27 '80		
APR 13 '81	APR 14 '81		
APR 30 '81	APR 27 '81		
OCT 10 '94	OCT 18 1994		
GAYLORD			PRINTED IN U.S.A.